MAY - - 2012

Careers in Focus

FINANCIAL SERVICES

FOURTH EDITION

Ferguson's
An Infobase Learning Company

Careers in Focus: Financial Services, Fourth Edition

Copyright © 2012 by Infobase Learning

Ferguson's
An imprint of Infobase Learning
132 West 31st Street
New York NY 10001

Library of Congress Cataloging-in-Publication Data

Careers in focus. Financial services. — 4th ed.
    p. cm.
  Includes bibliographical references and index.
  ISBN-13: 978-0-8160-8040-3 (hardcover : alk. paper)
  ISBN-10: 0-8160-8040-2 (hardcover : alk. paper)   1. Financial services
industry—Vocational guidance.   2. Finance—Vocational guidance.   I. Title:
Financial services.
  HG173.C285 2011
  332.023'73—dc23
                                                          2011020630

Ferguson's books are available at special discounts when purchased in bulk
quantities for businesses, associations, institutions, or sales promotions.
Please call our Special Sales Department in New York at (212) 967–8800 or
(800) 322–8755.

You can find Ferguson's on the World Wide Web at
http://www.infobaselearning.com

Text design by David Strelecky
Composition by Newgen North America
Cover printed by Yurchak Printing, Landisville, Pa.
Book printed and bound by Yurchak Printing, Landisville, Pa.
Date printed: October 2011
Printed in the United States of America

10 9 8 7 6 5 4 3 2 1

This book is printed on acid-free paper.

Table of Contents

Introduction

This guide to careers in the world of finance covers the accounting, banking, and insurance industries in detail. These industries have been undergoing constant change in recent years, primarily due to technological advances. Although the increased use of automation may cause some jobs to be phased out, there will be greater demand for workers who are knowledgeable about computers and information technology in addition to having financial skills and expertise.

Another important trend in accounting, banking, and insurance is the growth of involvement in international markets, particularly in Latin America and Asia. Those who have language skills and an interest in other cultures will have increasing opportunities to expand their career planning to other parts of the world.

Investment and financial planning services are also becoming an important part of financial services. The aging baby boomer population will seek advice from their accountants, banking professionals, and insurance representatives and require their services to plan a financially secure future.

Each article in this book discusses a particular financial services occupation in detail. The articles in *Careers in Focus: Financial Services* appear in Ferguson's *Encyclopedia of Careers and Vocational Guidance*, but have been updated and revised with the latest information from the U.S. Department of Labor, professional organizations, and other sources. The following paragraphs detail the sections and features that appear in the book.

The **Quick Facts** section provides a brief summary of the career including recommended school subjects, personal skills, work environment, minimum educational requirements, salary ranges, certification or licensing requirements, and employment outlook. This section also provides acronyms and identification numbers for the following government classification indexes: the Dictionary of Occupational Titles (DOT), the Guide for Occupational Exploration (GOE), the National Occupational Classification (NOC) Index, and the Occupational Information Network (O*NET)-Standard Occupational Classification System (SOC) index. The DOT, GOE, and O*NET-SOC indexes have been created by the U.S. government; the NOC index is Canada's career classification system. Readers can use the identification numbers listed in the Quick Facts section to access further information about a career. Print editions of the DOT (*Dictionary of Occupational Titles*. Indianapolis, Ind.: JIST Works,

1991) and GOE (*Guide for Occupational Exploration*. Indianapolis, Ind.: JIST Works, 2001) are available at libraries. Electronic versions of the DOT (http://www.oalj.dol.gov/libdot.htm), NOC (http://www5.hrsdc.gc.ca/NOC), and O*NET-SOC (http://www.onet online.org) are available on the Internet. When no DOT, GOE, NOC, or O*NET-SOC numbers are listed, this means that the U.S. Department of Labor or Human Resources and Skills Development Canada have not created a numerical designation for this career. In this instance, you will see the acronym "N/A," or not available.

The **Overview** section is a brief introductory description of the duties and responsibilities involved in this career. Oftentimes, a career may have a variety of job titles. When this is the case, alternative career titles are presented. Employment statistics are also provided, when available. The **History** section describes the history of the particular job as it relates to the overall development of its industry or field. **The Job** describes the primary and secondary duties of the job. **Requirements** discusses high school and post-secondary education and training requirements, any certification or licensing that is necessary, and other personal requirements for success in the job. **Exploring** offers suggestions on how to gain experience in or knowledge of the particular job before making a firm educational and financial commitment. The focus is on what can be done while still in high school (or in the early years of college) to gain a better understanding of the job. The **Employers** section gives an overview of typical places of employment for the job. **Starting Out** discusses the best ways to land that first job, be it through the college career services office, newspaper ads, Internet employment sites, or personal contact. The **Advancement** section describes what kind of career path to expect from the job and how to get there. **Earnings** lists salary ranges and describes the typical fringe benefits. The **Work Environment** section describes the typical surroundings and conditions of employment—whether indoors or outdoors, noisy or quiet, social or independent. Also discussed are typical hours worked, any seasonal fluctuations, and the stresses and strains of the job. The **Outlook** section summarizes the job in terms of the general economy and industry projections. For the most part, Outlook information is obtained from the U.S. Bureau of Labor Statistics and is supplemented by information gathered from professional associations. Job growth terms follow those used in the *Occupational Outlook Handbook*. Growth described as "much faster than the average" means an increase of 20 percent or more. Growth described as "faster than the average" means an increase of 14 to 19 percent. Growth described as "about as fast as the average" means an increase of 7 to 13 percent. Growth described as "more slowly than the average" means an increase of 3 to 6 percent. "Little or no change" means a decrease of 2 percent to an increase of 2 percent. "Decline" means a decrease of 3 percent or more. Each article ends with **For More Information,** which lists organizations that provide information on training, education, internships, scholarships, and job placement.

Careers in Focus: Financial Services also includes photos, informative sidebars, and interviews with professionals in the field.

Accountants and Auditors

OVERVIEW

Accountants compile, analyze, verify, and prepare financial records, including profit and loss statements, balance sheets, cost studies, and tax reports. Accountants may specialize in areas such as auditing, tax work, cost accounting, budgeting and control, or systems and procedures. Accountants also may specialize in a particular business or field; for example, *agricultural accountants* specialize in drawing up and analyzing financial statements for farmers and for farm equipment companies. *Auditors* examine and verify financial records to ensure that they are accurate, complete, and in compliance with federal laws. There are approximately 1.3 million accountants and auditors employed in the United States.

HISTORY

Accounting records and bookkeeping methods have been used from early history to the present. Records discovered in Babylonia (modern-day Iraq) date back to 3600 B.C., and accounts were similarly kept by the Egyptians, Greeks, and Romans.

Modern accounting began with the technique of double-entry bookkeeping, which was developed in the 15th and 16th centuries by Luca Pacioli, an Italian mathematician. After the Industrial Revolution, business grew more complex. As government and industrial institutions developed in the 19th and 20th centuries, accurate records and information were needed to assist in making decisions on economic and management policies.

The accounting profession in the United States dates back only to 1880, when English and Scottish investors began buying stock in American companies. To keep an eye on their investments, they sent over accountants who realized the great potential that existed in the accounting field and stayed on to establish their own businesses.

Federal legislation, such as the income tax in 1913 and the excess profits tax in 1917, helped cause an accounting boom that has made the profession instrumental to all business.

Accountants have long been considered "bean counters," and their work has been written off by outsiders as routine and boring. However, their image, once associated with death, taxes, and bad news, is making a turnaround. Accountants now do much more than prepare financial statements and record business transactions. Technology now counts the "beans," allowing accountants to analyze and interpret the results. Their work has expanded to encompass challenging and creative tasks such as computing costs and efficiency gains of new technologies, participating in strategies for mergers and acquisitions, supervising quality management, and designing and using information systems to track financial performance.

THE JOB

Accountants' duties depend on the size and nature of the company in which they are employed. The major fields of employment are public accounting, private accounting, government accounting, and internal auditing.

Public accountants work independently on a fee basis or as members of an accounting firm, and they perform a variety of tasks for businesses or individuals. These may include auditing accounts and records, preparing and certifying financial statements, conducting financial investigations and furnishing testimony in legal matters, and assisting in formulating budget policies and procedures.

Private accountants, sometimes called *industrial* or *management accountants,* handle financial records of the firms at which they are employed.

Government accountants work on the financial records of government agencies or, when necessary, they audit the records of private companies. In the federal government, many accountants are employed as *bank examiners, Internal Revenue Service agents and investigators,* as well as in regular accounting positions.

Within these fields, accountants can specialize in a variety of areas.

General accountants supervise, install, and devise general accounting, budget, and cost systems. They maintain records, balance books, and prepare and analyze statements on all financial aspects of a business. Administrative officers use this information to make sound business decisions.

Budget accountants review expenditures of departments within a firm to make sure expenses allotted are not exceeded. They also aid in drafting budgets and may devise and install budget control systems.

Cost accountants determine unit costs of products or services by analyzing records and depreciation data. They classify and record all operating costs so that management can control expenditures.

Property accountants keep records of equipment, buildings, and other property owned or leased by a company. They prepare mortgage schedules and payments as well as appreciation or depreciation statements, which are used for income tax purposes.

Environmental accountants help utilities, manufacturers, and chemical companies set up preventive systems to ensure environmental compliance and provide assistance in the event that legal issues arise.

Systems accountants design and set up special accounting systems for organizations whose needs cannot be handled by standardized procedures. This may involve installing automated or computerized accounting processes and includes instructing personnel in the new methods.

Forensic accountants and auditors use accounting principles and theories to support or oppose claims being made in litigation. (See the article Forensic Accountants and Auditors for more information.)

Tax accountants prepare federal, state, or local tax returns of an individual, business, or corporation according to prescribed rates, laws, and regulations. They also may conduct research on the effects of taxes on firm operations and recommend changes to reduce taxes. This is one of the most intricate fields of accounting, and many accountants therefore specialize in one particular phase such as corporate, individual income, or property tax.

Assurance accountants help improve the quality of information for clients in assurance services areas such as electronic commerce, risk assessment, and elder care. This information may be financial or nonfinancial in nature.

Auditors ensure that financial records are accurate, complete, and in compliance with federal laws. To do so they review items in original entry books, including purchase orders, tax returns, billing statements, and other important documents. Auditors may also prepare financial statements for clients and suggest ways to improve productivity and profits. *Internal auditors* conduct the same kind of examination and evaluation for one particular company. Because they are salaried employees of that company, their financial audits then must be certified by a qualified independent auditor. Internal auditors also review procedures and controls, appraise the efficiency and effectiveness of operations, and make sure their companies comply with corporate policies and government regulations.

Tax auditors review financial records and other information provided by taxpayers to determine the appropriate tax liability. State and federal tax auditors usually work in government offices, but they may perform a field audit in a taxpayer's home or office.

Revenue agents are employed by the federal government to examine selected income tax returns and, when necessary, conduct field audits and investigations to verify the information reported and adjust the tax liability accordingly.

Chief bank examiners enforce good banking practices throughout a state. They schedule bank examinations to ensure that financial institutions comply with state laws and, in certain cases, they take steps to protect a bank's solvency and the interests of its depositors and shareholders. (For more information, see the article Bank Examiners.)

REQUIREMENTS

High School

If you are interested in an accounting career, you must be very proficient in arithmetic and basic algebra. Familiarity with computers and their applications is equally important. Course work in English and communications will also be beneficial.

Postsecondary Training

Postsecondary training in accounting may be obtained in a wide variety of institutions such as private business schools, junior colleges, universities, and correspondence schools. A bachelor's degree with a major in accounting, or a related field such as economics, is highly recommended by professional associations for those entering the field and is required by all states before taking the licensing exam. It is possible, however, to become a successful accountant by completing a program at any of the above-mentioned institutions. A four-year college curriculum usually includes about two years of liberal arts courses, a year of general business subjects, and a year of specific accounting work. Better positions, particularly in public accounting, require a bachelor's degree with a major in accounting. Large public accounting firms often prefer people with a master's degree in accounting, or with a master's degree in business administration with a concentration in accounting. For beginning positions in accounting, the federal government requires four years of college (including 24 semester hours in accounting or auditing) or an equivalent combination of education and experience.

Certification or Licensing

A large percentage of all accountants and auditors are certified. Certified public accountants (CPAs) must pass a qualifying examination and hold a certificate issued by the state in which they wish to practice. In most states, a college degree is required for admission to the CPA examinations; a few states allow candidates to substitute years of public accounting experience for the college degree requirement. Currently all states (except California, Colorado, New Hampshire, and Vermont) and the District of Columbia require CPA candidates to have 150 hours of education, which is an additional 30 hours beyond the standard bachelor's degree. These criteria can be met by combining an undergraduate accounting program with graduate study or participating in an integrated five-year professional accounting program. You can obtain information from your state board of accountancy or check out the Web site of the American Institute of Certified Public Accountants (AICPA) to read about new regulations and review last year's exam.

The Uniform CPA Examination administered by the AICPA is used by all states. Nearly all states require at least two years of public accounting experience or its equivalent before a CPA certificate can be earned.

The AICPA offers additional credentialing programs (involving a test and additional requirements) for members with valid CPA certificates. These designations include accredited in business valuation, certified information technology professional, and personal financial specialist. These credentials indicate that a CPA has developed skills in nontraditional areas in which accountants are starting to play larger roles.

Some accountants seek out other credentials. Those who have earned a bachelor's degree, pass a four-part examination, agree to meet continuing education requirements, and have at least two years of experience in management accounting may become a certified management accountant through the Institute of Management Accounting.

The Accreditation Council for Accountancy and Taxation confers the following designations: accredited business accountant, accredited tax preparer, accredited tax adviser, and accredited retirement adviser.

To become a certified internal auditor, college graduates with two years of experience in internal auditing must pass a four-part examination given by the Institute of Internal Auditors (IIA). The IIA also offers the following specialty certifications: certified financial services auditor, certified government auditing professional, and certification in control self-assessment. Visit the IIA Web site for more information.

The designation certified information systems auditor is conferred by ISACA to candidates who pass an examination and who have five years of experience auditing electronic data processing systems.

Other organizations, such as BAI, confer specialized auditing designations.

Other Requirements

To be a successful accountant you will need strong mathematical, analytical, and problem-solving skills. You need to be able to think logically and to interpret facts and figures accurately. Effective oral and written communication skills are also essential in working with both clients and management.

Other important skills are attentiveness to detail, patience, and industriousness. Business acumen and the ability to generate clientele are crucial to service-oriented businesses, as are honesty, dedication, and a respect for the work of others.

EXPLORING

The American Institute of Certified Public Accountants offers an excellent Web site, http://www.startheregoplaces.com, which will help you learn more about the field. It features information on recommended high school courses, important personal skills for accountants, postsecondary training programs, scholarships, internships, and career options in the field.

If you think a career as an accountant or auditor might be for you, try working in a retail business, either part time or during the summer. Working at the cash register or even pricing products as a stockperson is good introductory experience. You should also consider working as a treasurer for a student organization requiring financial planning and money management. It may be possible to gain some experience by volunteering with local groups such as religious organizations and small businesses. You should also stay abreast of news in the field by reading trade magazines and checking out the industry Web sites of the AICPA and other accounting associations. The AICPA has numerous free educational publications available.

EMPLOYERS

Approximately 1.3 million people are employed as accountants and auditors. Accountants and auditors work throughout private industry and government. About 24 percent work for accounting, tax preparation, bookkeeping, and payroll services firms. Approximately 8 percent are self-employed. Others work as professors at colleges and universities.

STARTING OUT

Junior public accountants usually start in jobs with routine duties such as counting cash, verifying calculations, and other detailed numerical work. In private accounting, beginners are likely to start as cost accountants and junior internal auditors. They may also enter in clerical positions as cost clerks, ledger clerks, and timekeepers or as trainees in technical or junior executive positions. In the federal government, most beginners are hired as trainees at the GS-5 level after passing the civil service exam.

Some state CPA societies arrange internships for accounting majors, and some offer scholarships and loan programs.

You might also visit the Career Planning and Development section (http://www.aicpa.org/InterestAreas/YoungCPANetwork/Resources/ Networking/Pages/Planning_Developing.aspx) of the AICPA Web site. It has detailed information on accounting careers, hiring trends, job search strategies, resumes and cover letters, and job interviews. The section also has a list of internship opportunities for students.

ADVANCEMENT

Talented accountants and auditors can advance quickly. Junior public accountants usually advance to senior positions within several years and to managerial positions soon after. Those successful in dealing with top-level management may eventually become supervisors, managers, and partners in larger firms or go into independent practice. However, only 2 to 3 percent of new hires advance to audit manager, tax manager, or partner.

Private accountants in firms may become audit managers, tax managers, cost accounting managers, or controllers, depending on their specialty. Some become treasurers or corporation presidents. Others on the finance side may rise to become managers of financial planning and analysis or treasurers.

Federal government trainees are usually promoted within a year or two. Advancement to controller and to higher administrative positions is ultimately possible.

Although advancement may be rapid for skilled accountants, especially in public accounting, those with inadequate academic or professional training are often assigned to routine jobs and find it difficult to obtain promotions. All accountants find it necessary to continue their study of accounting and related areas in their spare time. Even those who have already obtained college degrees, gained experience, and earned a CPA certificate may spend many hours studying to keep up with new industry developments. Thousands of practicing accountants enroll in formal courses offered by universities and professional associations to specialize in certain areas of accounting, broaden or update their professional skills, and become eligible for advancement and promotion.

EARNINGS

Accountants with a bachelor's degree earned average starting salaries of $48,993 a year in July 2009, according to the National Association of Colleges and Employers. Those with master's degrees received starting salaries of $49,786.

According to the U.S. Department of Labor (DOL), accountants and auditors had median annual earnings of $60,340 in 2009. The lowest paid 10 percent earned less than $37,690, and the highest paid 10 percent earned more than $104,450. The DOL reports the following mean annual salaries for accountants and auditors by employer: federal government, $88,190; accounting, tax preparation, bookkeeping, and payroll services, $73,920; management of companies and enterprises, $66,630; insurance carriers, $65,520; local government, $57,490; and state government, $54,040.

Accountants and auditors receive typical benefits including paid vacation and sick days, insurance, and savings and pension plans. Employees in smaller companies generally receive fewer fringe benefits. Self-employed accountants and auditors must provide their own benefits.

WORK ENVIRONMENT

Accounting is known as a desk job, and a 40-hour (or longer) work-week can be expected in public and private accounting. Although computer work is replacing paperwork, the job can be routine and monotonous, and concentration and attention to detail are critical. Public accountants experience considerable pressure during the tax period, which runs from November to April, and they may have to work long hours. There is potential for stress aside from tax season, as accountants can be responsible for managing multimillion-dollar finances with no margin for error. Self-employed accountants and those working for a small firm can expect to work longer hours; 40 percent work more than 50 hours per week, compared to 20 percent of public and private accountants.

In smaller firms, most of the public accountant's work is performed in the client's office. A considerable amount of travel is often necessary to service a wide variety of businesses. In a larger firm, however, an accountant may have very little client contact, spending more time interacting with the accounting team.

OUTLOOK

Employment of accountants and auditors is expected to grow much faster than the average for all occupations through 2018, according to the DOL. This is due to business growth, changing tax and finance laws, and increased scrutiny of financial practices across all businesses. There have been several notable scandals in the accounting industry in recent years, and this accounts for much of the increased scrutiny and changing legislation in this industry.

As firms offer more specialized services, accountants will need to follow suit. Firms will seek out accountants with experience in marketing and proficiency in computer systems to build management consulting practices. As trade increases, so will the demand for CPAs with international specialties and foreign language skills. CPAs with an engineering degree would be well equipped to specialize in environmental accounting. Other accounting specialties that will enjoy good prospects include assurance and forensic accounting.

The number of CPAs dropped off a bit after most states embraced the 150-hour standard for CPA education. However, numbers are once again starting to rise as students realize the many opportunities this industry holds, especially in the wake of recent accounting scandals. CPAs with valid licenses should experience favorable job prospects for the foreseeable future. Pursuing advanced degrees and certifications will also greatly increase one's chances of finding employment.

Accounting jobs are more secure than most during economic downswings. Despite fluctuations in the nation's economy, there will always be a need to manage financial information, especially as the number, size, and complexity of business transactions increases. However, competition for jobs will remain, certification requirements will become more rigorous, and accountants and auditors with the highest degrees will be the most competitive.

FOR MORE INFORMATION

For information on accreditation and testing, contact
Accreditation Council for Accountancy and Taxation
1010 North Fairfax Street
Alexandria, VA 22314-1574
Tel: 888-289-7763
E-mail: info@acatcredentials.org
http://www.acatcredentials.org

For information on the Uniform CPA Examination and education and careers, contact
American Institute of Certified Public Accountants
1211 Avenue of the Americas
New York, NY 10036-8775
Tel: 212-596-6200
http://www.aicpa.org

For information on accredited programs in accounting, contact
Association to Advance Collegiate Schools of Business
777 South Harbour Island Boulevard, Suite 750
Tampa, FL 33602-5730
Tel: 813-769-6500
http://www.aacsb.edu

For information on certification for bank auditors, contact
BAI
115 South LaSalle Street, Suite 3300
Chicago, IL 60603-3801
Tel: 800-224-9889
E-mail: info@bai.org
http://www.bai.org

For information on women in accounting, contact
Educational Foundation for Women in Accounting
136 South Keowee Street
Dayton, OH 45402-2241
Tel: 937-424-3391
E-mail: info@efwa.org
http://www.efwa.org

For information on internal auditing and certification, contact
Institute of Internal Auditors
247 Maitland Avenue
Altamonte Springs, FL 32701-4201
Tel: 407-937-1100
E-mail: iia@theiia.org
http://www.theiia.org

For information about management accounting and the CMA designation, contact
Institute of Management Accountants
10 Paragon Drive, Suite 1
Montvale, NJ 07645-1718
Tel: 800-638-4427
E-mail: ima@imanet.org
http://www.imanet.org

For information on certification, contact
ISACA
3701 Algonquin Road, Suite 1010
Rolling Meadows, IL 60008-3124
Tel: 847-253-1545
http://www.isaca.org

INTERVIEW

Mitchell Freedman is a certified public accountant (CPA) and the founder and president of Mitchell Freedman Accountancy Corporation and MFAC Financial Advisors Inc. He has received many honors during his career, including the Distinguished Service Award from the Personal Financial Planning Section of the American Institute of Certified Public Accountants, and he was named as one of the "250 Best Financial Advisors" in the United States for five consecutive years by Worth *magazine. Mitchell has coauthored the*

Guide to Planning for Performing and Creative Artists and the Guide to Planning for Divorce. *He is a founder and past chair of California Jump$tart Coalition (http://www.cajumpstart.org), a nonprofit organization that seeks to improve the financial literacy of California youth. Mitchell discussed his career and the field of accounting with the editors of* Careers in Focus: Financial Services.

Q. What made you want to enter this career?

A. I wasn't originally drawn to the accounting profession. It was suggested to me by my uncle, and my parents urged me to pursue it also. I majored in accounting in college and I did well in my courses. I was particularly drawn by the numbers, which always meant more to me than mere statistics. I was able to see things in a very clear way when they were numerically quantified. I liked "the order" of numbers. The debits = credits also meant a lot to me. Some have said that being born under the Libra sign was one of the reasons that I was drawn to accounting. I must frankly admit that even after graduation from college I wasn't really clear on what accountants did. It was only after working and advancing in the field that I was able to piece together all of the various skill sets and experiences that are the accounting profession.

Q. What is one thing that young people may not know about a career in accounting?

A. Most people think of auditing and taxes when they think about a career in accounting. However, the path to an accounting career has many crossroads, turns, and a variety of aspects that can be undertaken. There is the public accountant, the auditor who issues opinions on financial statements for third-party use. There is the tax professional (with various areas in which someone can specialize). There is the internal accountant, the controller, vice president of finance, chief financial officer, etc. Then there are other areas such as forensic accounting, financial planning, and valuation accounting. The term *accountant* can encompass a broad array of experiences. But, what is "the one thing"? The designation, CPA (certified public accountant) is not just a credential, it is a license granted by a state board of accountancy. Accounting is a regulated profession.

Q. What are the most important personal and professional qualities for CPAs?

A. The most important quality is having an unbiased attitude (independence when doing an audit) so that the work done is always in the best interest of the third parties who would rely on your client's financial statements. One needs to have and exhibit a high degree of morality and ethics. One also must be self-motivated to do an outstanding job for the client, whatever role the CPA takes in his or her career. One must try to avoid conflicts of interest and be independent in fact as well as in appearance.

Q. What are some of the pros and cons of your job?

A. First, the "bad news." It's hard work. Regardless of the path you take you are generally always plagued with deadlines: the time that the audit report must be issued to the Securities and Exchange Commission, the due dates for tax returns, a client needs something done . . . yesterday.

The pros? It is a rewarding profession. One can make a very good living and be in a career where your skills are in demand by a large variety of prospective employers. Another pro is that one can advance as far as one's skill and ambition will take them. Still another pro is that you don't have to be buttonholed—you can go where your interests take you. One of the tenets of being an accountant is to commit to "life-long learning." Not only is there mandatory continuing education to keep your license current, the changes in laws, practices, businesses, and technology force you to commit to continue to be educated.

Q. What advice would you give to young people who are interested in the field?

A. Go for it. I recommend starting as an auditor because that is the one "franchise" that the CPA license grants to a practitioner. It will also help you develop the basic knowledge that will enable you to go anywhere in the field of business. It is the core of being an accountant. Also, don't limit yourself to going to "The Big Four" [Pricewaterhouse Coopers, Ernst & Young, Deloitte Touche Tohmatsu, and KPMG International]. Even a small CPA firm can provide you with a broad array of experiences and professional rewards. I started with a very small accounting firm and in my 46 years of practice I have only held four jobs. In three of them I became an owner, including my current firms [that] I started in 1981.

Q. What is the future employment outlook for CPAs? How is the field changing?

A. Technology is the change-agent in the accounting profession. New software and hardware allow accountants to provide services higher up in the value chain because the computer can take on the more mundane tasks typically thought to be accounting. It was not too many years ago that the CEO of the American Institute of Certified Public Accountants said that the CPA "brand" was too narrow and it wasn't elastic. He was so wrong, as CPAs provide such a broad array of services to clients, employers, government, and academia. The license is highly expandable. I have used my license to establish two successful and atypical financial services companies, and my education and prior experience truly aided me in my professional journey. CPAs are generally perceived as "the most trustworthy" professional in business and for good reason.

Q. Can you tell us about your work with California Jump$tart?

A. About 15 years ago a group of interested parties from business, government, quasi-government, not-for-profit, media, and educational organizations realized that our nation's financial illiteracy was a drag on our economy and a burden to society. We started a coalition of all of these groups with the mission to improve the financial literacy of California's youth (K–12). I have served on the board of CAJ$ since its inception, and I'm a past chair of the organization. The recent "Great Recession" that we have been plodding through has shown the havoc that financial illiteracy can bring to not only individuals and their families—but to our nation, indeed the global economy. We will not be satisfied until all of society has developed the skills to be able to understand and execute budgets and understand saving, managing credit, investments, retirement planning, education planning, etc. While we have had many successes, we have a long way to go.

Actuaries

OVERVIEW

Actuaries use statistical formulas and techniques to calculate the probability of events such as death, disability, sickness, unemployment, retirement, and property loss. Actuaries develop formulas to predict how much money an insurance company will pay in claims, which determines the overall cost of insuring a group, business, or individual. Increase in risk raises potential cost to the company, which, in turn, raises its rates. Actuaries analyze risk to estimate the number and amount of claims an insurance company will have to pay. They assess the cost of running the business and incorporate the results into the design and evaluation of programs.

Casualty actuaries specialize in property and liability insurance, *life actuaries* in health and life insurance. *Pension actuaries* deal only with pension plans. The total number of actuaries employed in the United States is approximately 19,700.

HISTORY

The term *actuary* was used for the first time in 1762 in the charter for the Equitable Society of London, which was the first life insurance company to use scientific data in figuring premiums. The basis of actuarial work was laid in the early 17th century when Frenchmen Blaise Pascal and Pierre de Fermat derived an important method of calculating actuarial probabilities, resulting in what is now termed the science of probability.

The first mortality table was produced in the late 17th century, when Edmund Halley noticed the regularity of various social phenomena, including the excess of male over female births. Halley, an English astronomer for whom Halley's comet is named, is known as the father of life insurance. As more complex forms of insurance were developed in the 19th century, the need for actuaries grew.

In 1889, a small group of qualified actuaries formed the Actuarial Society of America. Two classes of members, fellows and associates, were created seven years later, and special examinations were developed to determine membership eligibility. Forms of these examinations are still used today. By 1909 the American Institute of Actuaries was created, and in 1949 these two groups consolidated into the present Society of Actuaries.

In 1911, the Casualty Actuary Society was formed in response to the development of workers' compensation laws. The compensation laws opened up many new fields of insurance, and the Casualty Actuarial Society has since moved into all aspects of property and liability insurance.

OASDI (Old Age, Survivors, and Disability Insurance), now known as Social Security, was created in 1935 and expanded the work of pension actuaries. The creation of this program greatly impacted the development, philosophy, and structure of private pension programs. The American Society of Pension Actuaries (now known as the American Society of Pension Professionals & Actuaries) was formed in 1966; its members provide services to more than 30 percent of the qualified retirement plans in the United States.

The first actuaries were concerned primarily with statistical, mathematical, and financial calculations needed in the rapidly growing field. Today they deal with problems of investment, selection of risk factors for insurance, agents' compensation, social insurance, taxation, development of policy forms, and many other aspects of insurance. Once considered mathematicians, actuaries are now referred to as "financial architects" and "social mathematicians" because they use their unique combination of numerical, analytical, and business skills to solve a variety of social and financial problems.

THE JOB

Should smokers pay more for their health insurance? Should younger drivers pay higher car insurance premiums? Actuaries answer questions like these to ensure that insurance and pension organizations can pay their claims and maintain a profitable business.

Using their knowledge of mathematics, probability, statistics, and principles of finance and business, actuaries determine premium rates and the various benefits of insurance plans. To accomplish this task, they first assemble and analyze statistics on birth, death, marriage, parenthood, employment, and other pertinent facts and figures. Based on this information, they are able to develop mathematical models of rates of death, accident, sickness, disability, or retirement and then construct tables regarding the probability of such things as property loss from fire, theft, accident, or natural disaster. After calculating all probabilities and the resulting costs to the company, the actuaries can determine the premium rates to allow insurance companies to cover predicted losses, turn a profit, and remain competitive with other businesses.

For example, based on analyses, actuaries are able to determine how many of each 1,000 people 21 years of age are expected to survive to age 65. They can calculate how many of them are expected to die this year or how many are expected to live until age 85. The probability that an insured person may die during the period before reaching 65 is a risk to the company. The actuaries must figure a price for the premium that will cover all claims and expenses as they occur and still earn a profit for the company assuming the risk. In the same way, actuaries calculate premium rates and determine policy provisions for every type of insurance coverage.

Employment opportunities span across the variety of different types of insurance companies, including life, health, accident, automobile, fire, or workers' compensation organizations. Most actuaries specialize either as casualty actuaries, dealing with property and liability insurance, or as life actuaries, working with life and health insurance. In addition, actuaries may concentrate on pension plan programs sponsored and administered by various levels of government, private business, or fraternal or benevolent associations.

Actuaries work in many departments in insurance companies, including underwriting, group insurance, investment, pension, sales, and service. In addition to their own company's business, they analyze characteristics of the insurance business as a whole. They study general economic and social trends as well as legislative, health, and other developments, all of which may affect insurance practices. With this broad knowledge, some actuaries reach executive positions, where they can influence and help determine company policy and develop new lines of business. *Actuary executives* may communicate with government officials, company executives, policyholders, or the public to explain complex technical matters. They may testify before public agencies regarding proposed legislation that has a bearing on the insurance business, for example, or they may explain proposed changes in premium rates or contract provisions.

Actuaries may also work with a consulting firm, providing advice to clients including insurance companies, corporations, hospitals, labor unions, and government agencies. They develop employee benefits, calculating future benefits and employer contributions, and set up pension and welfare plans. *Consulting actuaries* also advise health care and financial services firms, and they may work with small insurance companies lacking an actuarial department.

Since the government regulates the insurance industry and administers laws on pensions, it also requires the services of actuaries to determine whether companies are complying with the law. A small number of actuaries are employed by the federal government and deal with Social Security, Medicare, disability and life insurance, and pension plans for veterans, members of the armed forces, and federal employees. Those in state governments may supervise and regulate insurance companies, oversee the operations of state retirement or pension systems, and manage problems related to unemployment insurance and workers' compensation.

REQUIREMENTS

High School
If you are interested in this field, you should pursue a traditional college preparatory curriculum including mathematical and computer science classes and also take advantage of advanced courses such as calculus. Introductory business, economics, accounting, and finance courses are important, as is English to develop your oral and written skills.

Postsecondary Training
A bachelor's degree with a major in actuarial science, mathematics, statistics, or a business-related field such as economics, finance, or business is highly recommended for entry into the industry. Courses in elementary and advanced algebra, differential and integral calculus, descriptive and analytical statistics, principles of mathematical statistics, probability, and numerical analysis are all important. Computer science is also a vital part of actuarial training. Employers are increasingly hiring graduates with majors in economics, business, and engineering who have a strong math background. College students should broaden their education to include business, economics, and finance as well as English and communications. Because actuarial work revolves around social and political issues, course work in the humanities and social sciences will also prove useful.

Certification or Licensing

Full professional status in an actuarial specialty is based on completing a series of 10 examinations. Success is based on both formal and on-the-job training. Actuaries can become associate members of the Society of Actuaries after successfully completing seven of the 10 examinations for the life and health insurance, finance, and pension fields. Similarly, they can reach associate status in the Casualty Actuarial Society after successfully completing seven out of 10 exams in the property and liability field. Most actuaries achieve associateship in three to five years. Actuaries who successfully complete the entire series of exams for either organization are granted full membership and become fellows.

The American Society of Pension Professionals and Actuaries also offers several different designations (both actuarial and non-actuarial) to individuals who pass the required examinations in the pension field and have the appropriate work experience.

Consulting pension actuaries who service private pension plans must be enrolled and licensed by the Joint Board for the Enrollment of Actuaries (http://www.irs.gov/taxpros/actuaries), a U.S. government agency. Only these actuaries can work with pension plans set up under the Employee Retirement Income Security Act. To be accepted, applicants must meet certain professional and educational requirements stipulated by the Joint Board.

Completion of the entire series of exams may take from five to 10 years. Because the first exams offered by these various boards and societies cover core material (such as calculus, linear algebra, probability and statistics, risk theory, and actuarial math), students generally wait to commit to a specialty until they have taken the initial tests. Students pursuing a career as an actuary should complete the first two or three preliminary examinations while still in college, since these tests cover subjects usually taught in school; the more advanced examinations cover aspects of the profession itself.

Employers prefer to hire individuals who have already passed the first two exams. Once employed, companies generally give employees time during the workday to study. They may also pay exam fees, provide study materials, and award raises upon an employee's successful completion of an exam.

Other Requirements

An aptitude in mathematics, statistics, and computer science is a must to become a successful actuary, as are sound analytical and problem-solving skills. Solid oral and written communication skills are also required in order to be able to explain and interpret complex work to the client.

Prospective actuaries should also have an inquisitive mind with an interest in historical, social, and political issues and trends. You should have a general feel for the business world and be able to assimilate a wide range of complex information in order to see the "big picture" when planning policies. Actuaries like to solve problems; they are strategists who enjoy and generally excel at games such as chess. Actuaries need to be motivated and self-disciplined to concentrate on detailed work, especially under stress, and to undertake the rigorous study for licensing examinations.

EXPLORING

If you think you are interested in the actuarial field, try pursuing extracurricular opportunities that allow you to practice strategic thinking and problem-solving skills; these may include chess, math, or investment clubs at your school. Other activities that foster leadership and management, such as student council positions, will also be beneficial. Any kind of business or research-oriented summer or part-time experience will be valuable, especially with an accounting or law firm.

There are many local actuarial clubs and regional affiliates throughout the United States that offer opportunities for informal discussion and networking. Talk with people in the field to better understand the nature of the work, and use the association's resources to learn more about the field. The Society of Actuaries offers free educational publications, including *The Future Actuary,* which is copublished with the Casualty Actuarial Society.

College undergraduates can take advantage of summer internships and employment in insurance companies and consulting firms. Students will have the chance to rotate among jobs to learn various actuarial operations and different phases of insurance work.

EMPLOYERS

There are approximately 19,700 actuaries employed in the United States, and about 55 percent work in the insurance industry. Approximately 16 percent of actuaries work for management, scientific and technical consulting services. Other actuaries work for financial service-providing firms including commercial banks, investment banks, and retirement funds. Others are employed in academia. Some actuaries are self-employed.

STARTING OUT

The best way to enter this field is by taking the necessary beginning examinations while still in college. Once students have graduated and passed these exams, they are in a very good position to apply for entry-level jobs in the field and can command higher starting salaries. Some college students organize interviews and find jobs through their college career services office, while others interview with firms recruiting on campus. Many firms offer summer and year-round actuarial training programs or internships that may result in a full-time job.

Beginning actuaries may prepare calculations for actuarial tables or work with policy settlements or funds. With experience, they may prepare correspondence, reports, and research. Beginners who have already passed the preliminary exams often start with more responsibility and higher pay.

ADVANCEMENT

Advancement within the profession to assistant, associate, or chief actuary greatly depends on the individual's on-the-job performance, competence on the actuarial examinations, and leadership capabilities.

Some actuaries qualify for administrative positions in underwriting, accounting, or investment because of their broad business knowledge and specific insurance experience. Because their judgment is so valuable, actuaries may advance to administrative or executive positions, such as head of a department, vice president or president of a company, manager of an insurance rating bureau, partner in a consulting firm, or, possibly, state insurance commissioner. Actuaries with management skills and a strong business background may move into other areas such as marketing, advertising, and planning.

EARNINGS

Starting salaries for actuaries with bachelor's degrees in actuarial science averaged $56,320 in July 2009, according to a survey conducted by the National Association of Colleges and Employers. New college graduates who have not passed any actuarial examinations earn slightly less. Insurance companies and consulting firms offer merit increases or bonuses to those who pass examinations.

The U.S. Department of Labor (DOL) reports that actuaries earned a median annual salary of $87,210 in 2009. Ten percent earned less than $51,950, while the top 10 percent earned more than $158,240. Actuaries working for insurance companies receive paid vacations, health and life insurance, pension plans, and other fringe benefits.

WORK ENVIRONMENT

Actuaries spend much of their 40-hour workweek behind a desk poring over facts and figures, although some travel to various units of the organization or to other businesses. This is especially true of the consulting actuary, who will most likely work longer hours and travel more. Consulting actuaries tend to have more diverse work and more personal interaction in working with a variety of clients. Though the work can be stressful and demands intense concentration and attention to detail, actuaries find their jobs to be rewarding and satisfying and feel that they make a direct and positive impact on people's lives.

OUTLOOK

The DOL predicts that employment for actuaries will grow much faster than the average for all occupations through 2018. The insurance industry—the leading employer of actuaries—is expected to experience some growth, with many new fields such as annuities and terrorism-related property-risk analysis, compensating for the shrinking life insurance industry and declining demand for pension actuaries.

The insurance industry continues to evolve, and actuaries will be in demand to establish rates in several new areas of coverage, including prepaid legal, dental, and kidnapping insurance. In many cases, actuarial data that have been supplied by rating bureaus are now being developed in new actuarial departments created in companies affected by states' new competitive rating laws. Other new areas of insurance coverage that will involve actuaries include product and pollution liability insurance, as well as greater workers' compensation and medical malpractice coverage. Insurers will call on actuaries to help them respond to new state and federal regulations while cutting costs, especially in the areas of pension reform and no-fault automobile insurance. In the future, actuaries will also be employed by noninsurance businesses or will work in business- and investment-related fields. Some are already working in banking and finance.

Actuaries will be needed to assess the financial impact of current issues such as AIDS, terrorism, and the changing health care system. As demographics change, people live and work longer, and as medicine advances, actuaries will need to re-examine the probabilities of death, sickness, and retirement.

Casualty actuaries will find more work as companies find themselves held responsible for product liability. In the wake of recent environmental disasters, such as the BP oil leak in the Gulf of Mexico, there will also be a growing need to evaluate environmental risk.

Opportunities will be best for those in the consulting industry as companies continue to outsource their risk analysis needs. Opportunities should also be strong for actuaries in the heath care industry.

As business goes global, it presents a whole new set of risks and problems as economies develop and new markets emerge. As private enterprise expands in the former Soviet Union, how does a company determine the risk of opening, say, a department store in Moscow?

Actuaries are no longer just mathematical experts. With their unique combination of analytical and business skills, their role is expanding as they become broad-based business professionals solving social as well as financial problems.

FOR MORE INFORMATION

For general information about actuary careers, contact
American Academy of Actuaries
1850 M Street, NW, Suite 300
Washington, DC 20036-5805
Tel: 202-223-8196
http://www.actuary.org

For information about continuing education and professional designations, contact
American Society of Pension Professionals and Actuaries
4245 North Fairfax Drive, Suite 750
Arlington, VA 22203-1648
Tel: 703-516-9300
E-mail: asppa@asppa.org
http://www.asppa.org

The Be An Actuary section of the CAS Web site offers comprehensive information on the career of actuary.

Casualty Actuarial Society (CAS)
4350 North Fairfax Drive, Suite 250
Arlington, VA 22203-1620
Tel: 703-276-3100
E-mail: office@casact.org
http://www.casact.org
http://www.beanactuary.org

For information about a career as a consulting actuary, contact
Conference of Consulting Actuaries
3880 Salem Lake Drive, Suite H
Long Grove, IL 60047-5292
Tel: 847-719-6500
E-mail: conference@ccactuaries.org
http://www.ccactuaries.org

For information about continuing education and professional
designations, contact
Society of Actuaries
475 North Martingale Road, Suite 600
Schaumburg, IL 60173-2265
Tel: 847-706-3500
http://www.soa.org

For information on careers in Canada, contact
Canadian Institute of Actuaries
800-150 Metcalfe Street
Ottawa, ON K2P 1P1 Canada
Tel: 613-236-8196
http://www.actuaries.ca

INTERVIEW

Jeff Kucera, FCAS, MAAA, is a senior actuarial consultant in the
Chicago office of EMB America, an actuarial consultancy firm.
(EMB America will soon become part of Towers Watson.) He has
worked in the field for 35 years. Jeff discussed his career with the
editors of Careers in Focus: Financial Services.

Q. What made you want to enter this career?
A. As a senior in high school I visited the University of Nebraska,
where we were given the opportunity to visit with a number of

department heads. One of the areas that I had elected to visit was actuarial science, which at that time was headed by Steve Kellison. His description of the field and the job opportunities [that were available] were very impressive. Because I liked both math and business, but did not want to go into teaching or accounting, actuarial science seemed like it would be a good fit.

Q. What are a few things that young people may not know about a career in actuarial science?

A. There are a lot of things that young people may not know or understand about actuarial science and a career in general, but I will concentrate on just a couple of things. First, as you pursue the exams and a career in actuarial science you will learn a lot about insurance other than just the mathematics of insurance pricing. You will learn a lot about insurance law, policy contracts, claim and sales practices, etc. All of this helps actuaries develop a very broad perspective of the business, and much broader than most other disciplines. It is one of the reasons that many companies seek the advice and opinions of actuaries about a number of topics, and not just pricing opinions.

Second, while actuaries typically start off their career in actuarial science, many branch off to other areas—never to return. This is because of this broad perspective that they develop early in their careers, while taking actuarial exams. One of the major areas drawing actuarial talent is the product management areas, where the product manager is given the top- and bottom-line responsibility for either a line of business and/or geographical area.

Q. What are some of the pros and cons of your job?

A. The pros and cons are generally what you make them. The biggest pros for me are the different people you get to work with and the wide variety of assignments. Other pros would be the respect you typically get from coworkers, fairly good employment rates, very decent salaries, etc. There are obviously some good reasons that the career of actuary typically is ranked as one of the top three job professions.

The biggest con would probably be taking the licensing exams. This is a major commitment, and generally comes right out of college. For most of us it is not a real short time, i.e., it is going to be five to 10 years upon graduation from college before you are through with all the exams. While the rewards for finishing the exams are very satisfactory, it is not something that should be approached lightly.

Q. **What are the most important personal and professional qualities for people in your career?**

A. The most important personal and professional qualities will vary somewhat from individual to individual, and what track their career follows. Probably the one thing that is critical for everyone when they first enter this field is the ability to pass the exams and persevere through this time. It will take a lot of patience, and the ability to bounce back after failing an exam, which most of us have done at least once before achieving our final goal. And for many people thinking about entering the profession, exam failure is something that they never had to face before. The exam process can definitely be a little humbling for many of us, especially when first starting out.

After that I think one of the more important traits for people in this career is the ability to communicate, first with their peer group and then with non-actuaries. This second audience can be more difficult to communicate with because frequently they are not familiar with a lot of "actuarial jargon" and so the challenge can be to take complex theories or ideas and describe them in simplified language so that other members of the company, or the general public, can understand the concept and importance of what is being done.

Q. **What activities would you suggest to high school students who are interested in this career?**

A. Get involved with outside activities and begin developing your leadership skills. It might be as a member of a school club—that hopefully leads to being an officer of such club or part of a volunteer organization. These types of activities can help develop both your leadership and communication skills. Joining clubs and striving for leadership roles should help develop your overall leadership skills. Hopefully it will also improve other skills, such as listening to what other people have to say and what is important to them, negotiating between disagreeing parties, learning to explain and sell your own ideas, dealing with disappointments when your suggestions/ideas are declined, etc.

Volunteering in different activities can also be a great way to improve your communication skills, particularly if it is an area in which you may not originally have a lot of familiarity. If you are doing a good job you have to listen closely to what is being asked and required. Also, it can help you to begin realizing that not everyone has the same perspective/outlook on things. Understanding and learning to appreciate different perspectives can be extremely helpful in the business world. Sales, claims, underwriting, actuarial, etc. all have a different way of viewing and perceiving situations that arise in the business world. Learning to understand these different perspectives will help you to better negotiate with different departments and also to develop the best integrated approach to problems.

Q. What advice would you give to young people who are interested in the field?

A. Get started early. It helps if you can decide that this is the field you want to be in as a senior in high school, and can start out your college career with this focus.

Don't get discouraged during the exams. It is highly unlikely that you will go through all the exams without some failure. Remember, most everyone entering this field has typically been one of the top math students in their high school class. Now all of these students are taking the same test, and that test will be graded on a curve where only 40 to 50 percent may pass. You will likely have some failures.

Understand the commitment you are making. Unlike many of your friends, after four years of college their studying is pretty much over; your studying is just beginning. You will be expected to spend 100 to 200 hours of your own time (this is over and above time you may be given on your job) studying for a particular exam. It can be a drag, but the rewards are pretty good at the end. This additional time commitment is why some people have compared becoming a fellow in the Casualty Actuarial Society or the Society of Actuaries equivalent to getting a Ph.D.

Take as many business courses to supplement your math and actuarial science classes as possible. Also, if your school offers any type of insurance courses, make sure that you sign up for those. This will help supplement your actuarial background and also help you develop a more rounded view of the industry.

Have fun. Any career you choose will be greatly affected by your attitude and disposition towards the job. Approach your career with the attitude that it is a great one and that you are going to have fun doing the work, and you will enjoy it immensely.

Bank Examiners

OVERVIEW

Bank examiners investigate financial institutions to ensure their safety and soundness and to enforce federal and state laws. They arrange audits, review policies and procedures, study documents, and interview managers and employees. They prepare detailed reports that can be used to strengthen banks.

A bank examiner's fundamental duty is to make sure people do not lose the money they have entrusted to banks. Bank examiners protect account holders. They also protect the federal and state governments that are responsible for insuring financial institutions. There are approximately 27,000 financial examiners employed in the United States.

HISTORY

The First Bank of the United States, founded in Philadelphia in 1791, was an unqualified success. It acted as the federal government's banker and received private and business deposits. The bank issued banknotes that could be exchanged for gold and succeeded in creating a national currency. In 1811, the visionary experiment came to an untimely end; despite the bank's many successes, its charter was not renewed. In a time when states' rights were considered supreme, a national bank was an unpopular idea.

The second national bank fared just as well—and no better. Despite an impressive list of achievements, the bank failed when President Andrew Jackson vetoed its charter renewal.

For the next several decades, the nation adhered to a system of "free banking," meaning that bank charters were readily granted to groups that met limited standards. The number of state banks multiplied rapidly. Each state bank issued its own banknotes, creating an untenable currency system.

In the 1860s, the U.S. Civil War destroyed the South's economy. Banks in the southern states did not have the resources to weather the difficulties. The only national financial organization, the Independent Treasury, was ill equipped to meet the ensuing financial demands. The price of "free banking" became painfully clear.

In 1864, as the nation struggled to rebuild itself, the federal government passed the National Bank Act. Intended to bring about economic stability and prevent future bank failures, the act created the Office of the Comptroller of the Currency (OCC). The OCC initially had the power to charter national banks that could issue national banknotes. The OCC also was the first organization to conduct bank examinations.

Unfortunately, the National Bank Act of 1864 did not bring about the desired stability. Over the next several decades, the country experienced four bank panics, the worst of which occurred in 1907. Bank panics were characterized by "runs on the banks," during which people became fearful and tried to withdraw all their money, all at once. The banks often did not have enough cash in reserve and many failed. The Federal Reserve Act (1913) created a centralized reserve system that could lend banks money and prevent bank crises.

In its early form, the Federal Reserve System was unable to prevent the bank failures that led, in 1929, to the Great Depression. In 1933, in response to the Depression, the Federal Reserve's powers were extended. The Federal Reserve eventually would become a central bank that actively promoted monetary stability. Like the OCC, the Federal Reserve now regularly examines banks.

The Federal Deposit Insurance Corporation (FDIC) also was created in 1933. The FDIC pays depositors if an insured bank closes without the resources to repay people their money. The FDIC also is charged with the responsibility of preventing unsound banking practices within the banks it insures. The FDIC regularly examines all the banks it insures in order to ensure their safety and soundness. Since its creation, the FDIC has successfully prevented any widespread bank panics.

The years since 1933 have seen many challenges. In the mid-1980s, hundreds of savings and loan banks failed, reinforcing the need for the regular, thorough examination of banks by the OCC, the Federal Reserve, the FDIC, and a number of other federal and state agencies. In 2007, a shortfall in liquid assets and financial mismanagement (which included high-risk lending practices) by some

Top Federal Government Agencies

There are many opportunities with the federal government for people who are interested in financial services careers. The Partnership for Public Service and American University's Institute for the Study of Public Policy Implementation surveys federal workers every few years regarding job satisfaction and engagement. In its 2010 survey, it found that the overall employee satisfaction score for all government agencies was 65.0 (out of a top score of 100). Here are some of the large federal financial agencies that ranked higher than the average:

Agency	Rank in 2010	Score
Government Accountability Office	#2	81.6
Federal Deposit Insurance Corporation	#3	79.2
Social Security Administration	#6	71.6
Department of the Treasury	#12	68.4
Department of Commerce	#13	68.3

banks and other financial institutions caused a worldwide financial crisis. Some banks in the United States closed; others needed financial bailouts from the U.S. government. Many called this financial crisis the worst since the Great Depression. These developments underscore the need for strong monitoring of our nation's financial institutions. Today, most banks are examined on an annual basis, often by more than one regulatory organization.

THE JOB

When most people think of bank examiners, they envision the examiner from *It's a Wonderful Life*—a humorless bureaucrat who threatens to destroy George Bailey. In reality, bank examiners are public servants. They work to ensure that our nation's banks remain strong and safe. Essentially, they protect our money and our nation's economy.

A bank examiner's primary responsibilities are to ensure the safety and soundness of the bank he or she examines and to enforce the rules and regulations of the state or federal organization he or she represents. To accomplish this, bank examiners travel to different banks throughout the year. In most small- to medium-sized banks, they set up temporary offices. In larger banks, they may have permanent offices. The examination process can take anywhere from a few weeks to several months, depending on the size of the bank. A few extremely large banks are examined constantly throughout the year.

Bank examiners should not be confused with auditors or accountants. A bank examiner is as interested in a bank's operations as in the bank's financial records. Bank examiners conduct their examinations by reviewing a bank's policies to see, first of all, whether the policies are sound. They then review the bank's records to discover whether the bank is following its own policies. Bank examiners also observe the bank's day-to-day operations and interview managers and employees.

Ed Seifried, who served as a bank examiner within the OCC for more than 25 years, notes, "Bank examinations should involve dialogue and discussion. Banks may not like the process [of being examined], but they generally accept it if they feel that they are being assessed by people who treat them fairly and who understand banking."

Bank examiners usually work in teams under one bank-examiner-in-charge. Each member or group within a team studies a different area of the bank's operations. One person or group might study the bank's lending policies and procedures. Another might study the bank's asset management. Still others examine the bank's information technology or estate management. Different regulatory agencies examine different types of banks and different areas of operation. The *chief bank examiner* assembles the team for each bank. The composition of these teams varies depending on the nature of each bank's business. Because banking practices today are so complex, many regulatory organizations design their examination strategy around a bank's greatest areas of risk. This so-called supervision by risk enables regulatory organizations to examine banks more frequently and with greater efficiency.

"Every examination is tailored to the individual bank," says Seifried. "The person in charge of the exam studies the bank in advance in order to develop an examination strategy."

Once a team of examiners has thoroughly reviewed different areas of a bank's operations, they analyze their findings, draw conclusions, and prepare a report. This report is forwarded to the regulatory agency for review. It is then returned to the bank's board of directors. These reports wield considerable power. A bank must act quickly to correct any problems identified in an examination. If a bank fails to do so, bank examiners have the authority to exact fines. In severe cases, a bank examiner can close banks or insist that they merge with other, more sound banks.

Because bank examiners must be able to exercise completely independent judgment about a bank's operations, their reports are strictly confidential. "The confidentiality is to ensure that there is no interference with the regulatory process," Seifried explains. "If bank examiners could be sued for rendering judgments, they might not be able to be as objective."

REQUIREMENTS

High School

If you are interested in entering this profession, you should begin laying a solid college prep foundation during high school. Take math courses, such as algebra and geometry, statistics, and business courses. Also, take as many computer courses as you can. You will be using computers throughout your career, and the more comfortable you are with this tool the better. You should also take English classes to develop good writing and communication skills. Researching, compiling reports, and presenting your findings will be a large part of your job as a bank examiner.

Postsecondary Training

After high school, the next step on your road to becoming a bank examiner is to get a college degree. Typical majors for this field include accounting, economics, business administration, commercial or banking law, or other business-related subjects. Once you have graduated from college, you may choose to work immediately for a regulatory agency or you may gain applied business experience by working, for example, for a financial institution. Either option is acceptable, though more and more regulatory agencies are actively recruiting candidates who have some business experience. Another possibility is to complete your education while working at the same time through such programs as the OCC's Bank Examiner Cooperative Education Program (see the Web site http://www .occ.gov/about/careers/index-careers.html). Remember, though, that whatever route you pick, you will not become a full-fledged bank examiner overnight. Those who begin their careers working for a regulatory agency generally start as assistant or associate examiners.

If you enter the field after gaining business experience, you may start at a higher-level position, but it will still take some time and training to become a bank examiner.

Regulatory agencies provide rigorous training for their bank examiners. Assistant bank examiners must take a series of courses and tests during their first several years as employees of a regulatory agency. They also gain on-the-job experience by working on examination teams. To become a bank examiner, you will need five or more years of experience in auditing or examining financial institutions. In addition, candidates with the best potential for advancement have experience with evaluating computer risk management in financial institutions. That is, they have a great deal of knowledge about assessing the security and flexibility of a financial institution's computer system.

Certification or Licensing

Some employers require their employees have or give promotion preference to employees with industry certifications, such as certified financial analyst (offered by the CFA Institute) or certified information systems auditor (offered by ISACA). In addition, bank examiners must be commissioned (approved) to examine banks only by a state or federal regulator before they can function as full-fledged examiners. This process typically takes five years. BAI, an organization for financial professionals, also offers a number of courses that can help individuals prepare for careers as examiners.

Other Requirements

Successful bank examiners are committed to lifelong learning. Even after you have reached the position of bank examiner, it will be important to stay on top of new computer developments, laws and regulations, and changes in the field. Also, you should be able to work well with others since you will be working with teams of examiners as well as interacting with professionals at the financial institutions being examined. Be prepared to travel as part of your job; often you will be sent from one financial institution to another to perform examinations. Finally, if you enjoy detailed and analytical work with numbers, this may be the field for you.

EXPLORING

A good way to learn more about this field is by conducting information interviews with various banking professionals. You also should read all the literature banks produce in order to learn about different types of accounts and saving mechanisms.

College students should seek part-time jobs or internships within banks. Because bank examiners must be familiar with banking operations from the ground up, one of the best places for a college student to gain experience is by working as a teller in a bank.

EMPLOYERS

Approximately 27,000 financial examiners are employed in the United States. Almost all bank examiners are employees of federal or state governing agencies. They work for the Office of the Comptroller of the Currency (OCC), the Federal Reserve System, the Office of Thrift Supervision, the Federal Deposit Insurance Corporation, and many other federal and state agencies.

STARTING OUT

College graduates can enter this field via a number of avenues. The Office of Personnel Management (OPM) is the federal government's human resources department. The OPM maintains a list of job listings and also can provide information about requirements, benefits, and salaries. Visit http://www.usajobs.opm.gov for more information.

Someone interested in this work should also contact an agency, such as the OCC, directly and apply for openings. Most federal regulatory agencies, and many state agencies, maintain job hotlines and Web sites. (For examples on the Web, visit the Careers at the OCC page, http://www.occ.gov/about/careers/index-careers.html and the Careers at FDIC page, http://www.fdic.gov/about/jobs.)

A number of private newsletters available in print or online, such as *Federal Career Opportunities* (http://www.fedjobs.com) and *Federal Jobs Digest* (http://www.jobsfed.com) also list federal job openings.

ADVANCEMENT

Individuals usually enter this field as assistant examiners and, over the course of four to five years, progress to *commissioned examiners*. Commissioned examiners might be given responsibility for several small banks. As the examiner gains experience and establishes a reputation for integrity, insight, and thoroughness, he or she may be given responsibility for larger banks and larger teams of examiners. Examiners who handle larger banks also tend to earn more money.

After many years, an examiner may be offered a supervisory position. *Supervisors* usually stay in one office and are responsible for managing a large number of examiners who are working in the field.

Examiners also advance by moving to agencies that offer higher salary scales. Still others leave the profession entirely and put their skills to work as *banking consultants*. Because examiners study so many different banks, of varying degrees of soundness and efficiency, they can become highly successful, sought-after consultants.

EARNINGS

According to the U.S. Department of Labor (DOL), the mean salary of financial examiners who worked for the federal government was $101,650, while those employed by state agencies earned $60,990. The top paid 10 percent of all financial examiners earned $129,620 or more. The lowest paid 10 percent earned less than $40,680.

Most state and federal employees receive excellent benefits, such as health insurance, dental and vision coverage, life insurance, retirement packages, savings plans, sick leave, paid holidays, disability insurance, and child care allowance. The benefits for government employees tend to be extremely competitive and difficult to match in the private sector.

WORK ENVIRONMENT

A bank examiner is a nomadic creature, spending several weeks or months in each location before moving on. Bank examiners often work closely with teams of up to 30 or 40 other examiners who also are separated from their family and friends. Most examination teams develop a strong sense of camaraderie that sustains them during the weeks they must live out of hotels. To compensate for the travel, many regulatory agencies offer examiners an extra day off every other week. Examiners who work in these agencies work nine business days and take the 10th day off.

Bank examiners work in temporary offices, surrounded by professionals who may harbor ambiguous feelings about being examined. The work, however, can be interesting and rewarding.

"It can be a great job," says Ed Seifried. "I was with the OCC for more than 25 years and I spent 23 of those years in the field. I loved that part of it. When you're in the field, you are surrounded by knowledgeable people who have a strong interest in getting problems resolved. You also have a lot of interesting conversations."

OUTLOOK

The DOL predicts that employment for financial examiners will grow much faster than the average for all occupations through 2018.

The recent financial crisis has prompted government agencies at the state and federal levels to more closely monitor the activities of banks. As a result, more examiners will be needed. This prediction for strong growth may be offset somewhat if the trend toward bank mergers and closings continues.

Those who decide to become bank examiners can expect considerable job security. Employment in this field is usually not affected by general economic fluctuations. In addition, job openings will result from the need to replace those who retire or leave for other positions.

FOR MORE INFORMATION

The BAI is an organization for financial professionals offering such things as seminars, training courses, and Banking Strategies *magazine.*
   BAI
   115 South LaSalle Street, Suite 3300
   Chicago, IL 60603-3801
   Tel: 800-224-9889
   E-mail: info@bai.org
   http://www.bai.org

The Federal Reserve System influences money and credit conditions in the United States, supervises and regulates banking, maintains the stability of the financial system, and provides certain financial services. For banking news, career opportunities, and publications, visit its Web site.
   Board of Governors of the Federal Reserve System
   20th Street and Constitution Avenue, NW
   Washington, DC 20551-0001
   Tel: 202-452-3000
   http://www.federalreserve.gov

The Federal Deposit Insurance Corporation (FDIC) is responsible for maintaining public confidence in the nation's banking system. The FDIC provides deposit insurance for banks and savings associations. This resource can offer information about banking policies, regulations, and career opportunities.
   Federal Deposit Insurance Corporation (FDIC)
   3501 North Fairfax Drive
   Arlington, VA 22226-3599
   Tel: 877-275-3342
   E-mail: publicinfo@fdic.gov
   http://www.fdic.gov

The Federal Reserve Bank of Minneapolis is one of the 12 Federal Reserve Banks throughout the United States. This source can provide information about the economy, the history of banking in the United States, and career opportunities within the Federal Reserve.
Federal Reserve Bank of Minneapolis
90 Hennepin Avenue
Minneapolis, MN 55401-1804
Tel: 612-204-5000
http://www.minneapolisfed.org

The Office of Personnel Management is the primary human resources center for the U.S. government. This resource can provide additional information about requirements, training, opportunities, and salaries.
Office of Personnel Management
1900 E Street, NW
Washington, DC 20415-1000
Tel: 202-606-1800
http://www.opm.gov

The Office of the Comptroller of the Currency (OCC) supervises national banks to ensure a safe, sound, and competitive national banking system. This resource can offer information about the opportunities, training, requirements, and salary scale within the OCC.
Office of the Comptroller of the Currency (OCC)
Administrator of National Banks
Washington, DC 20219-0001
Tel: 800-613-6743
E-mail: publicaffairs3@occ.treas.gov
http://www.occ.treas.gov

The Office of Thrift Supervision (OTS) is the primary regulator of all federal and many state-chartered thrift institutions. This resource can offer information about the opportunities, training, requirements, and salary scale within the OTS.
Office of Thrift Supervision (OTS)
1700 G Street, NW
Washington, DC 20552-0003
Tel: 202-906-6000
E-mail: public.info@ots.treas.gov
http://www.ots.treas.gov

Bookkeeping and Accounting Clerks

OVERVIEW

Bookkeeping and accounting clerks record financial transactions for government agencies, businesses, and other organizations. They compute, classify, record, and verify numerical data in order to develop and maintain accurate financial records. There are approximately 2.1 million bookkeeping, accounting, and auditing clerks employed in the United States.

HISTORY

The history of bookkeeping developed along with the growth of business and industrial enterprise. The first known records of bookkeeping date back to 2600 B.C., when the Babylonians used pointed sticks to mark accounts on clay slabs. By 3000 B.C., Middle Eastern and Egyptian cultures employed a system of numbers to record merchants' transactions of the grain and farm products that were distributed from storage warehouses. The growth of intricate trade systems brought about the necessity for bookkeeping systems.

Sometime after the start of the 13th century, the decimal numeration system was introduced in Europe, simplifying bookkeeping record systems. The merchants of Venice—one of the busiest trading centers in the world at that time—are credited with the invention of the double entry bookkeeping method that is widely used today.

As industry in the United States expands and grows more complex, simpler and quicker bookkeeping methods and procedures

Learn More About It: Career Planning

Alba, Jason. *Vault Career Guide to Accounting.* 3d ed. New York: Vault Inc., 2008.

Gaylord, Gloria, and Glenda Ried. *Careers in Accounting.* 4th ed. New York: McGraw-Hill, 2006.

Loosvelt, Derek. *Vault Guide to the Top Financial Services Employers.* 5th ed. New York: Vault Inc., 2008.

Ring, Trudy. *Careers in Finance.* 3d ed. New York: McGraw-Hill, 2004.

Schrayer, Robert M. *Opportunities in Insurance Careers.* New York: McGraw-Hill, 2007.

Sumichrast, Michael, and Martin A. Sumichrast. *Opportunities in Financial Careers.* New York: McGraw-Hill, 2004.

have evolved. Technological developments include bookkeeping machines, computer hardware and software, and electronic data processing.

THE JOB

Bookkeeping workers keep systematic records and current accounts of financial transactions for businesses, institutions, industries, charities, and other organizations. The bookkeeping records of a firm or business are a vital part of its operational procedures because these records reflect the assets and the liabilities, as well as the profits and losses, of the operation.

Bookkeepers record these business transactions daily in spreadsheets on computer databases, and accounting clerks often input the information. The practice of posting accounting records directly onto ledger sheets, in journals, or on other types of written accounting forms is decreasing as computerized record keeping becomes more widespread. In small businesses, bookkeepers sort and record all the sales slips, bills, check stubs, inventory lists, and requisition lists. They compile figures for cash receipts, accounts payable and receivable, and profits and losses.

Accounting clerks handle the clerical accounting work; they enter and verify transaction data and compute and record various charges. They may also monitor loans and accounts payable and receivable. More advanced clerks may reconcile billing vouchers, while senior workers review invoices and statements.

Accountants set up bookkeeping systems and use bookkeepers' balance sheets to prepare periodic summary statements of financial transactions. Management relies heavily on these bookkeeping records to interpret the organization's overall performance and uses them to make important business decisions. The records are also necessary to file income tax reports and prepare quarterly reports for stockholders.

Bookkeeping and accounting clerks work in retail and wholesale businesses, manufacturing firms, hospitals, schools, charities, and other types of institutional agencies. Many clerks are classified as financial institution bookkeeping and accounting clerks, insurance firm bookkeeping and accounting clerks, hotel bookkeeping and accounting clerks, and railroad bookkeeping and accounting clerks.

General bookkeepers and *general-ledger bookkeepers* are usually employed in smaller business operations. They may perform all the analysis, maintain the financial records, and complete any other tasks that are involved in keeping a full set of bookkeeping records. These employees may have other general office duties, such as mailing statements, answering telephone calls, and filing materials. *Audit clerks* verify figures and may be responsible for sending them on to an audit clerk supervisor.

In large companies, an accountant may supervise a department of bookkeepers who perform more specialized work. *Billing and rate clerks* and *fixed capital clerks* may post items in accounts payable or receivable ledgers, make out bills and invoices, or verify the company's rates for certain products and services. *Account information clerks* prepare reports, compile payroll lists and deductions, write company checks or send payments electronically, and compute federal tax reports or personnel profit shares. Large companies may employ workers to organize, record, and compute many other types of financial information.

In large business organizations, bookkeepers and accountants may be classified by grades, such as bookkeeper I or II. The job classification determines their responsibilities.

REQUIREMENTS

High School

In order to be a bookkeeper, you will need at least a high school diploma. It will be helpful to have a background in business mathematics, business writing, typing, and computer training. Pay particular attention to developing sound English and communication skills along with mathematical abilities.

Postsecondary Training

Some employers prefer people who have completed a junior college curriculum or those who have attended a post–high school business training program. In many instances, employers offer on-the-job training for various types of entry-level positions. In some areas, work-study programs are available in which schools, in cooperation with businesses, offer part-time, practical on-the-job training combined with academic study. These programs often help students find immediate employment in similar work after graduation. Local business schools may also offer evening courses.

Certification or Licensing

The American Institute of Professional Bookkeepers offers voluntary certification to bookkeepers who have at least two years of full-time experience (or the part-time or freelance equivalent), pass an examination, and sign a code of ethics. Bookkeepers who complete this requirement may use the designation certified bookkeeper.

Other Requirements

Bookkeepers need strong mathematical skills and organizational abilities, and they have to be able to concentrate on detailed work. The work is quite sedentary and often tedious, and you should not mind long hours behind a desk. You should be methodical, accurate, and orderly and enjoy working on detailed tasks. Employers look for honest, discreet, and trustworthy individuals when placing their business in someone else's hands.

Once you are employed as a bookkeeping and accounting clerk, some places of business may require you to have union membership. Larger unions include the Office and Professional Employees International Union; the International Union of Electronic, Electrical, Salaried, Machine, and Furniture Workers-Communications Workers of America; and the American Federation of State, County, and Municipal Employees. Also, depending on the business, clerks may be represented by the same union as manufacturing employees.

EXPLORING

You can gain experience in bookkeeping by participating in work-study programs or by obtaining part-time or summer work in beginning bookkeeping jobs or related office work. Any retail experience dealing with cash management, pricing, or customer service is also valuable.

You can also volunteer to manage the books for extracurricular student groups. Managing income or cash flow for a club or acting as treasurer for student government are excellent ways to gain experience in maintaining financial records.

Other options are visiting local small businesses to observe their work and talking to representatives of schools that offer business training courses.

EMPLOYERS

Of the approximately 2.1 million bookkeeping, auditing, and accounting clerks, many work for personnel supplying companies; that is, those companies that provide part-time or temporary office workers. Approximately 25 percent of bookkeeping and accounting clerks work part time, according to the U.S. Department of Labor (DOL). Many others are employed by government agencies and organizations that provide educational, health, business, and social services.

STARTING OUT

You may find jobs or establish contacts with businesses that are interested in interviewing graduates through your guidance or career services offices. A work-study program or internship may result in a full-time job offer. Business schools and junior colleges generally provide assistance to their graduates in locating employment.

You may locate job opportunities by applying directly to firms or responding to ads in newspaper classified sections. State employment agencies and private employment bureaus can also assist in the job search process.

ADVANCEMENT

Bookkeeping workers generally begin their employment by performing routine tasks, such as the simple recording of transactions. Beginners may start as entry-level clerks, cashiers, bookkeeping machine operators, office assistants, or typists. With experience, they may advance to more complex assignments that include computer training in databases and spreadsheets and assume a greater responsibility for the work as a whole.

With experience and education, clerks become department heads or office managers. Further advancement to positions such as office or division manager, department head, accountant, or auditor is possible with a college degree and years of experience. There is a high turnover rate in this field, which increases the promotion opportunities for employees with ability and initiative.

EARNINGS

Earnings for bookkeeping and accounting clerks are influenced by such factors as the size of the city or town where they work, their skill set and educational background, and the size and type of business for which they are employed. According to the DOL, bookkeepers and accounting clerks earned a median annual income of $33,450 a year in 2009. Clerks just starting out earn approximately $21,280 or less. Those with one or two years of college generally earn higher starting salaries. Top-paying jobs averaged $50,450 or more a year.

Employees usually receive six to eight paid holidays yearly and one week of paid vacation after six to 12 months of service. Paid vacations may increase to four weeks or more, depending on length of service and place of employment. Fringe benefits may include health and life insurance, sick leave, and retirement plans.

WORK ENVIRONMENT

The majority of office workers, including bookkeeping professionals, usually work a 40-hour week, although some employees may work a 35- to 37-hour week. Bookkeeping and accounting clerks usually work in typical office settings. They are more likely to have a cubicle than an office. While the work pace is steady, it can also be routine and repetitive, especially in large companies where the employee is often assigned only one or two specialized job duties.

Attention to numerical details can be physically demanding, and the work can produce eyestrain and nervousness. While bookkeepers usually work with other people and sometimes under close supervision, they can expect to spend most of their day behind a desk; this may seem confining to people who need more variety and stimulation in their work. In addition, the constant attention to detail and the need for accuracy can place considerable responsibility on the worker and cause much stress.

OUTLOOK

A growing number of financial transactions and the implementation of the Sarbanes-Oxley Act of 2002, which requires more accurate reporting of financial data for public companies, has created steady employment growth for bookkeeping and accounting clerks. Employment of bookkeeping and accounting clerks is expected to grow about as fast as the average for all occupations through 2018, according to the DOL.

There will be numerous replacement job openings, since the turn-over rate in this occupation is high. Offices are centralizing their operations, setting up one center to manage all accounting needs in a single location. As more companies trim back their workforces, opportunities for temporary work should continue to grow.

The automation of office functions—including improvements in document-scanning technology and accounting software—will continue to increase overall worker productivity, which may limit job growth in some settings. Excellent computer skills, skill in multiple bookkeeping and accounting activities, and professional certification will be vital to securing a job.

FOR MORE INFORMATION

For information on certification and career opportunities, contact
American Institute of Professional Bookkeepers
6001 Montrose Road, Suite 500
Rockville, MD 20852-4873
Tel: 800-622-0121
E-mail: info@aipb.org
http://www.aipb.org

For information on accredited educational programs, contact
Association to Advance Collegiate Schools of Business
777 South Harbour Island Boulevard, Suite 750
Tampa, FL 33602-5730
Tel: 813-769-6500
http://www.aacsb.edu

For information on women in accounting, contact
Educational Foundation for Women in Accounting
136 South Keowee Street
Dayton, OH 45402-2241
Tel: 937-424-3391
E-mail: info@efwa.org
http://www.efwa.org

For free office career and salary information, visit
OfficeTeam
http://www.officeteam.com

Commodities Brokers

QUICK FACTS

School Subjects
Agriculture
Business
Mathematics

Personal Skills
Communication/ideas
Leadership/management

Work Environment
Primarily indoors
Primarily one location

Minimum Education Level
High school diploma

Salary Range
$29,980 to $66,930 to
$1,000,000+

Certification or Licensing
Required

Outlook
About as fast as the average

DOT
162

GOE
10.02.02

NOC
1113

O*NET-SOC
41–3031.00, 41–3031.01

OVERVIEW

Commodities brokers, also known as *futures commission merchants,* act as agents in carrying out purchases and sales of commodities for customers or traders. Commodities are primary goods that are either raw or partially refined. Such goods are produced by farmers, such as corn, wheat, or cattle, or mined from the earth, such as gold, copper, or silver. Brokers, who may work at a brokerage house, on the floor of a commodities exchange, or independently, are paid a fee or commission for acting as the middleman to conduct and complete the trade. Approximately 317,200 securities, commodities, and financial services sales agents (a group including commodities brokers) are employed in the United States.

HISTORY

In medieval Europe, business was transacted at local market fairs, and commodities, primarily agricultural, were traded at scheduled times and places. As market fairs grew, "fair letters" were set up as a currency representing a future cash settlement for a transaction. With these letters, merchants could travel from one fair to another. This was the precursor to the Japanese system, in which landowners used "certificates of receipt" for their rice crops. As the certificates made their way into the economy, the Dojima Rice Market was established and became the first place where traders bought and sold contracts for the future delivery of rice.

"Forward contracts" entered the U.S. marketplace in the early 19th century. Farmers, swept up in the boom of industrial growth, transportation, and commerce, began to arrange for the future sale

48

A broker signals to a colleague to make a buy as trading takes place at the New York Mercantile Exchange. *(Monika Graff, The Image Works)*

of their crops. Traders entered the market along with the development of these contracts. However, there were no regulations to oversee that the commodity was actually delivered or that it was of an acceptable quality. Furthermore, each transaction was an individual business deal because the terms of each contract were variable. To address these issues, the Chicago Board of Trade was formed in 1848, and by 1865 it had set up standards and rules for trading "to arrive" contracts, now known as commodity futures contracts. In 2007, the Chicago Board of Trade merged with the Chicago Mercantile Exchange to become the CME Group.

THE JOB

A futures contract is an agreement to deliver a particular commodity, such as wheat, pork bellies, or coffee, at a specific date, time, and place. For example, a farmer might sell his oats before they are sowed (known as hedging) because he cannot predict what kind of price he will be able to demand later on. If the weather is favorable and crops are good, he will have competition, which will drive prices down. If there is a flood or drought, oats will be scarce, driving the price up. He wants to ensure a fair price for his product to protect his business and limit his risk, since he cannot predict what will happen.

On the other side of the equation is the user of the oats, perhaps a cereal manufacturer, who purchases these contracts for a delivery of oats at some future date. Producers and users do not correspond to a one-to-one ratio, and the broker is a middleman who does the buying and selling of contracts between the two groups. Brokers may place orders to buy or sell contracts for themselves, for individual clients, or for companies, all of which hope to make a profit by correctly anticipating the direction of a commodity's price. Brokers are licensed to represent clients, and brokers' first responsibility is to take care of their clients' orders before doing trading for themselves. *Traders* also buy and sell contracts for themselves. Unlike brokers, however, they are not licensed (and thus not allowed) to do this work for clients.

When placing a trade for others, brokers are paid a fee or a commission for acting as the agent in making the sale. There are two broad categories of brokers, though they are becoming less distinct. *Full service brokers* provide considerable research to clients, offer price quotes, give trading advice, and assist the customer in making trading decisions. *Discount brokers* simply fill the orders as directed by clients. Some brokers offer intermediate levels of optional services on a sliding scale of commission, such as market research and strategic advice.

In general, brokers are responsible for taking and carrying out all commodity orders and being available on call to do so; reporting back to the client upon fulfilling the order request; keeping the client abreast of breaking news; maintaining account balances and other financial data; and obtaining market information when needed and informing the client about important changes in the marketplace.

Brokers can work on the floor of a commodity futures exchange—the place where contracts are bought and sold—for a brokerage house or independently. The exchange has a trading floor where brokers transact their business in the trading pit. There are 10 domestic exchanges, with the main ones in Chicago, Kansas City, New York, and Minneapolis. To be allowed to work on the floor, a broker must have a membership (also known as a "seat") in the exchange or must be employed by a company with a seat in the exchange, which is a private organization. Memberships are limited to a specific number, and seats may be rented or purchased. Although seat prices vary due to factors such as the health of the overall economy and the type of seat being purchased, they are all extremely expensive. Seat prices can range from tens of thousands of dollars to hundreds of thousands of dollars (full seats have been known to sell for $700,000 and more). Naturally, this expense alone limits the number of individuals who can become members. In addition to being able to afford a seat, candidates for membership to any exchange must undergo thorough investigations of their credit standings, financial backgrounds, characters, and understanding of trading.

Most brokers do not have seats but work for brokerage houses that deal in futures. Examples of these houses include Merrill Lynch or Morgan Stanley, which deal in stocks, bonds, commodities, and other investments, and smaller houses, such as R. J. O'Brien and Associates LLC, that handle only commodities.

Companies can also have a seat on the exchange, and they have their own *floor brokers* in the pit to carry out trades for the brokerage house. Brokers in the company take orders from the public for buying or selling a contract and promptly pass it on to the floor broker in the pit of the exchange. *Specialists* or *market makers* also work on the exchange floor. According to the U.S. Department of Labor (DOL), "There is generally one for each security or commodity being traded. They facilitate the trading process by quoting prices and by buying or selling shares when there are too many or too few available." Brokers also have the choice of running their own business. Known as *introducing brokers,* they handle their own clients and trades and use brokerage houses to place their orders. Introducing brokers earn a fee by soliciting business trades, but they don't directly handle the customer's funds.

REQUIREMENTS
High School
Although there are no formal educational requirements for becoming a broker, a high school diploma and a college degree are strongly recommended. Commodities brokers need to have a wide range of knowledge, covering such areas as economics, world politics, and sometimes even the weather. To begin to develop this broad base of knowledge, start in high school by taking history, math, science, and business classes. Since commodities brokers are constantly working with people to make a sale, take English classes to enhance your communication skills. In addition to this course work, you might also consider getting a part-time job working in a sales position. Such a job will also give you the chance to hone your communication and sales skills.

Postsecondary Training
The vast majority of brokers have a college degree. While there is no "commodities broker major," you can improve your chances of

obtaining a job in this field by studying economics, finance, accounting, or business administration while in college. Keep in mind that you should continue to develop your understanding of politics and technologies, so government and computer classes will also be useful. Some commodities brokers also go on to earn master's degrees in business administration. Brokers also receive intensive on-the-job training from their employers after they are hired.

Brokerage firms look for employees who have sales ability, strong communication skills, and self-confidence. Commodities is often a second career for many people who have demonstrated these qualities in other positions.

Certification or Licensing

To become a commodities broker, it is necessary to pass the National Commodities Futures Examination (the Series 3 exam) to become eligible to satisfy the registration requirements of federal, state, and industry regulatory agencies. The test covers market and trading knowledge as well as rules and regulations and is composed of true/false and multiple-choice questions. Registration for the exam is through the Financial Industry Regulatory Authority (http://www.finra.org). Preparation materials are available through a number of sources, such as the Institute for Financial Markets (http://www.theifm.org). Brokers must also register with the National Futures Association.

Other Requirements

To be a successful broker, you must possess a combination of research and money management skills. You need to be attentive to detail and have a knack for analyzing data. Strong communication and sales skills are important as well, as brokers make money by convincing people to let them place their trades. An interest in and awareness of the world around you will also be a contributing factor to your success in this field, as commodities are influenced by everything from political decisions and international news to social and fashion trends.

You must also be emotionally stable to work in such a volatile environment. You need to be persistent, aggressive, and comfortable taking risks and dealing with failure. Strong, consistent, and independent judgment is also key. You must be a disciplined hard worker, able to comb through reams of market reports and charts to gain a thorough understanding of a particular commodity and the mechanics of the marketplace. You also need to be outspoken and assertive and able to yell out prices loudly and energetically on the trading floor (in settings where the open outcry format is still used) and to command attention.

EXPLORING

Students interested in commodities trading should visit one of the futures exchanges. All of them offer public tours, and you'll get to see up close just how the markets work and the roles of the players involved. All the exchanges offer educational programs and publications, and most have a Web site (see For More Information at the end of this article). The CME Group publishes *An Introduction to Futures and Options,* the full text of which is available at http://www.cmegroup.com/files/intro_fut_opt.pdf. There are hundreds of industry newsletters and magazines available (such *as Futures Magazine,* available at http://www.futuresmag.com), and many offer free samples of publications or products. Read what trading advisers have to say and how they say it. Learn their lingo and gain an understanding of the marketplace. If you have any contacts in the industry, arrange to spend a day with a broker. Watch him or her at work, and you'll learn how orders are entered, processed, and reported.

Do your own research. Adopt a commodity, chart its prices, test some of your own ideas, and analyze the marketplace. There are also a variety of inexpensive software programs, as well as Web sites, that simulate trading.

Finally, consider a job as a *runner* during the summer before your freshman year in college. Runners transport the order, or "paper," from the phone clerk to the broker in the pit and relay information to and from members on the floor. This is the single best way to get hands-on experience in the industry.

EMPLOYERS

Approximately 317,200 securities, commodities, and financial services sales agents (a group including commodities brokers) are employed in the United States. Commodities brokers work on the floor of a commodity futures exchange, for brokerage houses, or independently.

STARTING OUT

College graduates can start working with a brokerage house as an associate and begin handling stocks. After several years they can take the certification exam and move into futures. Another option is to start as support staff, either at the exchange or the brokerage house. Sales personnel try to get customers to open accounts, and account executives develop and service customers for the brokerage firm. At the exchange, *phone clerks* receive incoming orders and communicate the information to the runners. Working in the back as an accountant, money manager, or member of the research staff is also another route. College career services offices may be able to assist graduates in finding jobs with brokerage houses. Applications may also be made directly to brokerage houses.

Many successful brokers and traders began their careers as runners, and each exchange has its own training program. Though the pay is low, runners learn the business very quickly with a hands-on experience not available in an academic classroom. Contact one of the commodities exchanges for information on becoming a runner.

ADVANCEMENT

A broker who simply executes trades can advance to become a full-service broker. Through research and analysis and the accumulation of experience and knowledge about the industry, a broker can advance from an order filler and become a commodity trading adviser. A broker can also become a money manager and make all trading decisions for clients.

Within the exchange, a broker can become a *floor manager,* overseeing the processes of order taking and information exchange. To make more money, a broker can also begin to place his or her own trades for his or her own private account, though the broker's first responsibility is to the customers.

EARNINGS

This is an entrepreneurial business. A broker's commission is based on the number of clients he or she recruits, the amount of money they invest, and the profit they make. The sky's the limit. In recent years, the most successful broker made $25 million. A typical salary for a newly hired employee in a brokerage might average $1,500 per month plus a 30 percent commission on sales. Smaller firms are likely to pay a smaller commission. The DOL reports that the median annual earnings for securities, commodities, and financial services sales representatives (a group including commodities brokers) were $66,930 in 2009. The lowest paid 10 percent earned less than $29,980; the highest paid 25 percent earned more than $118,640 annually.

Benefits vary but are usually very good at large employers. For example, those working at one of the world's leading futures exchanges enjoy benefits such as vacation and sick days; medical, life, and disability insurance; and flextime during summer months.

Full tuition reimbursement may also be available, as well as a company-matched savings plan, a tax-deferred savings plan, and a pension program.

WORK ENVIRONMENT

A growing number of exchanges now use electronic systems to automate trades, and many use them exclusively. At exchanges that still use the "open outcry" system, the trading floor is noisy and chaotic. Every broker must be an auctioneer, yelling out his own price bids for purchases and sales. The highest bid wins and silences all the others. When a broker's primal scream is not heard, bids and offers can also be communicated with hand signals.

Brokers stand for most of the day, often in the same place, so that traders interested in their commodity can locate them easily. Each broker wears a distinctly colored jacket with a prominent identification badge. The letter on the badge identifies the broker and appears on the paperwork relating to the trade. Members of the exchange and employees of member firms wear red jackets. Some brokers and traders also have uniquely patterned jackets to further increase their visibility in the pit.

Brokers and traders do not have a nine-to-five job. While commodities trading on the exchange generally takes place from 9:00 A.M. to 1:00 P.M., international trading runs from 2:45 P.M. to 6:50 A.M.

In the rough and tumble world of the futures exchange, emotions run high as people often win or lose six- or seven-figure amounts within hours. Tension is fierce, the pace is frantic, and angry, verbal, and sometimes physical exchanges are not uncommon.

OUTLOOK

The DOL predicts that employment for securities, commodities, and financial services sales agents will grow about as fast as the average for all careers through 2018. Employment is expected to grow by 9 percent during this time span. The global financial crisis and the recession in the United States have caused the financial industry to contract, which has reduced the number of jobs for commodities brokers. Some growth will occur as a result of the growing number and increasing complexity of investment options and the new commodities available for investment due to the increasingly globalized marketplace. Additionally, as people and companies become more interested in and sophisticated about investing, they are entering futures markets and need the services provided by brokers. Baby Boomers are reaching retirement age, and many are looking to invest in markets as a way of saving for their futures; additionally, many women in the workforce and higher household incomes means more investment.

New computer and information technology is rapidly influencing and advancing the industry. Many systems have unique features designed specifically to meet customers' needs. New technology, such as electronic order entry, links to overseas exchanges, and night trading, is rapidly evolving, offering brokers new ways to manage risk and provide price information.

Because many people are attracted to this work by the possibility of earning large incomes, competition for jobs is particularly keen. However, job turnover is also fairly high due to the stress of the work and the fact that many beginning brokers are not able to establish a large enough clientele to be profitable. Small brokerage firms will offer the best opportunities for those just starting out in this work.

FOR MORE INFORMATION

This center provides information on workshops, home study courses, educational materials, and publications for futures and securities professionals.
Center for Futures Education
PO Box 309
Grove City, PA 16127-0309
Tel: 724-458-5860
E-mail: info@thectr.com
http://www.thectr.com

For a general overview of options, visit the CBOE Web site.
Chicago Board Options Exchange (CBOE)
400 South LaSalle Street
Chicago, IL 60605-1023
Tel: 877-843-2263
http://www.cboe.com

The CME Group was formed in 2007 as a result of a merger between the Chicago Mercantile Exchange and the Chicago Board of Trade. Visit its Web site for a wide variety of educational programs and materials, and general information on commodities careers.
CME Group
Tel: 800-331-3332
E-mail: info@cmegroup.com
http://www.cmegroup.com

For information on the commodities futures industry, contact
Commodity Futures Trading Commission
Three Lafayette Centre
1155 21st Street, NW
Washington DC 20581-0001
Tel: 202-418-5000
E-mail: questions@cftc.gov
http://www.cftc.gov

For more information on the National Commodities Futures Examination, contact
Financial Industry Regulatory Authority
1735 K Street
Washington, DC 20006-1500
Tel: 301-590-6500
http://www.finra.org

For information on membership, training, and registration, contact
National Futures Association
120 Broadway, #1125
New York, NY 10271-1196
Tel: 212-608-8660
E-mail: information@nfa.futures.org
http://www.nfa.futures.org

Visit the Web sites or contact the following exchanges for general background information about the field:
Intercontinental Exchange
https://www.theice.com

Minneapolis Grain Exchange
http://www.mgex.com

For information on the agricultural industry, contact
U.S. Department of Agriculture
1400 Independence Avenue, SW
Washington, DC 20250-0002
Tel: 202-720-2791
http://www.usda.gov

Credit Analysts

QUICK FACTS

School Subjects
Business
Computer science
Mathematics

Personal Skills
Communication/ideas
Leadership/management

Work Environment
Primarily indoors
Primarily one location

Minimum Education Level
Bachelor's degree

Salary Range
$34,420 to $57,470 to
$112,710+

Certification or Licensing
Voluntary

Outlook
Faster than the average

DOT
160

GOE
13.02.04

NOC
N/A

O*NET-SOC
13-2041.00

OVERVIEW

Credit analysts analyze financial information to evaluate the amount of risk involved in lending money to businesses or individuals. They contact banks, credit associations, and others to obtain credit information and prepare a written report of findings used to recommend credit limits. There are approximately 73,200 credit analysts employed in the United States.

HISTORY

Only 50 or 75 years ago, lending money was based mainly on a person's reputation. Money was lent after a borrower talked with friends and business acquaintances. Now, of course, much more financial background information is demanded. The use of credit cards and other forms of borrowing has skyrocketed in the last several years, and today, only accepted forms of accounting are used to determine if a loan applicant is a good risk. As business and financial institutions have grown more complex, the demand for professional credit analysis has also expanded.

THE JOB

Credit analysts typically concentrate on one of two different areas. *Commercial* and *business analysts* evaluate risks in business loans; *consumer credit analysts* evaluate personal loan risks. In both cases an analyst studies financial documents such as a statement of assets and liabilities submitted by the person or company seeking the loan and consults with banks and other financial institutions that have had previous financial relationships with the applicant. Credit analysts prepare, analyze, and approve loan requests and help borrowers fill out applications.

58

The scope of work involved in a credit check depends in large part on the size and type of the loan requested. A background check on a $3,000 car loan, for example, is much less detailed than on a $400,000 commercial improvement loan for an expanding business.

On the Web

There are many Web sites where you can find information on careers in finance, read financial news, and conduct company research. Listed here are a few that are important to people in the finance industry.

Bloomberg
http://www.bloomberg.com

Bloomberg Businessweek
http://www.businessweek.com

Business Finance
http://businessfinancemag.com

Careers in Finance
http://www.careers-in-finance.com

CNNMoney.com
http://money.cnn.com

Financial Times
http://www.ft.com/home/uk

Forbes
http://www.forbes.com

Fortune
http://money.cnn.com/magazines/fortune

Hoover's
http://www.hoovers.com

Institutional Investor
http://www.institutionalinvestor.com

TheStreet.com
http://www.thestreet.com

Vault
http://www.vault.com

Wall Street Journal
http://online.wsj.com

In both cases, financial statements and applicants will be checked by the credit analyst, but the larger loan will entail a much closer look at economic trends to determine if there is a market for the product being produced and the likelihood of the business failing. Because of these responsibilities, many credit analysts work solely with commercial loans.

In studying a commercial loan application, a credit analyst is interested in determining if the business or corporation is well managed and financially secure and if the existing economic climate is favorable for the operation's success. To do this, a credit analyst examines balance sheets and operating statements to determine the assets and liabilities of a company, its net sales, and its profits or losses. An analyst must be familiar with accounting and bookkeeping methods to ensure that the applicant company is operating under accepted accounting principles. A background check of the applicant company's leading officials is also done to determine if they personally have any outstanding loans. An on-site visit by the analyst may also be necessary to compare how the company's operations stack up against those of its competitors.

Analyzing economic trends to determine market conditions is another responsibility of the credit analyst. To do this, the credit analyst computes dozens of ratios to show how successful the company is in relation to similar businesses. Profit-and-loss statements, collection procedures, and a host of other factors are analyzed. This ratio analysis can also be used to measure how successful a particular industry is likely to be, given existing market considerations. Software programs are used to highlight economic trends and interpret other important data.

The credit analyst always provides a findings report to bank executives. This report includes a complete financial history of the applicant and usually concludes with a recommendation on the loan amount, if any, that should be advanced.

REQUIREMENTS

High School

If you are interested in this career, take courses in mathematics, economics, business, and accounting in high school. You should also take English courses to develop sound oral and written language skills. Computer science courses will help you to become computer literate, learn software programs, understand their applications to particular fields, and learn how to locate and access electronic information.

Postsecondary Training

Credit analysts usually have at least a bachelor's degree in accounting, finance, or business administration. Those who want to move up in the field often go on to obtain master's degrees in one of these subjects. Undergraduate course work should include business management, economics, statistics, and accounting. In addition, keep honing your computer skills. Some employers provide new hires with on-the-job training involving both classroom work and hands-on experience.

Certification and Licensing

The National Association of Credit Management offers the following voluntary certifications to credit professionals: credit business associate, credit business fellow, and certified credit executive. Contact the association for more information (see For More Information at the end of this article).

Other Requirements

To be a credit analyst, you should have an aptitude for mathematics and be adept at organizing, assessing, and reporting data. You must be able to analyze complex problems and devise resourceful solutions. Credit analysts also need strong interpersonal skills. You must be able to interview loan applicants and communicate effectively, establish solid working relationships with customers as well as coworkers, and clearly relate the results of your work.

EXPLORING

For the latest information on the credit management industry, check out newsgroups and Web pages on the Internet that are related to this field. For example, the National Association of Credit Management's Web site, http://www.nacm.org, has information about the field and links to other industry sites.

Consider a position as treasurer for student council or other student-run organizations. This will introduce you to the responsibilities associated with managing money. Or explore a part-time job as a bank clerk, teller, or customer service representative that will familiarize you with banking procedures. This is also a good way to network with professionals in the banking field. Various clubs and organizations may have opportunities for volunteers to develop experience working with budgets and financial statements. Join or start a business club at your school. Local institutions and small or single-owner businesses may welcome students interested in learning more about financial operations.

EMPLOYERS

Credit analysts are employed by banks, credit unions, credit agencies, business credit institutions, credit bureaus, corporations, and loan companies. They are also employed by hotels, hospitals, and department stores. Approximately 73,200 credit analysts are employed in the United States.

STARTING OUT

Although some people enter the field with a high school or two-year degree, most entry-level positions go to college graduates with degrees in fields such as accounting, finance, economics, and business administration. Credit analysts receive much of their formal training and learn specific procedures and requirements on the job. Many employees also rise through the ranks via other positions such as teller or customer service representative prior to becoming a credit analyst. Newspaper want ads, school career services offices, job search Web sites, and direct application to specific employers are all ways of tracking down that first job.

ADVANCEMENT

Credit analysts generally advance to supervisory positions. However, promotion and salary potential are limited, and many employees often choose to leave a company for better-paying positions elsewhere. After three to five years of credit work, a skilled credit analyst can expect a promotion to *credit manager* and ultimately *chief credit executive*. Responsibilities grow to include training other credit personnel, coordinating the credit department with other internal operations, and managing relations with customers and financial institutions.

EARNINGS

Salaries of credit analysts depend on the individual's experience and education. The size of the financial institution is also a determining factor: Large banks tend to pay more than smaller operations. Salaries also increase with the number of years in the field and with a particular company. According to the U.S. Department of Labor (DOL), credit analysts had a median annual income of $57,470 in 2009. The lowest paid 10 percent earned less than $34,420, and the highest paid 10 percent earned more than $112,710. Those in senior positions often have advanced degrees.

As an added perk, many banks offer their credit analysts free checking privileges and lower interest rates on personal loans. Other benefits include health insurance, sick and vacation pay, and retirement plans.

WORK ENVIRONMENT

Most credit analysts work in typical corporate office settings that are well lighted and air conditioned in the summertime. Credit analysts can expect to work a 40-hour week, but they may have to put in overtime if a project has a tight deadline. A commercial credit analyst may have to travel to the business or corporation that is seeking a loan in order to prepare the agreement. Credit analysts can expect heavy caseloads. Respondents to the annual survey of the National Association of Credit Management reported handling 250 to 2,000 active accounts per year.

A credit analyst should be able to spend long hours behind a desk quietly reading and analyzing financial reports. Attention to detail is critical. Credit analysts can expect to work in high-pressure situations, with loans of millions of dollars dependent on their analysis.

OUTLOOK

Employment in this field is expected to grow faster than the average for all occupations through 2018, according to the DOL. Credit analysts are crucial to the success and profitability of banks and other financial organizations, and the number, variety, and complexity of credit applications are on the rise. As the field of cash management grows along with the economy and the population, banks and other financial institutions will need to hire credit analysts. Opportunities should be best for those with strong educational backgrounds and those living in urban areas that tend to have the largest and greatest number of banks and other financial institutions.

Credit analysts are particularly busy when interest rates drop and applications for loans surge. Job security is influenced by the local economy and business climate. However, loans are a major source of income for banks, and credit officers are less likely than most workers to lose their jobs in an economic downturn.

Information technology is affecting the field of credit analysis as public financial information, as well as economic and market research, becomes more accessible via the Internet. Credit professionals now have a broader range of data available upon which to base decisions.

FOR MORE INFORMATION

For general banking industry information, contact
American Bankers Association
1120 Connecticut Avenue, NW
Washington, DC 20036-3902
Tel: 800-226-5377
http://www.aba.com

For publications and information on continuing education and training programs for financial institution workers, contact
BAI
115 South LaSalle Street, Suite 3300
Chicago, IL 60603-3801
Tel: 800-224-9889
E-mail: info@bai.org
http://www.bai.org

For information on the industry, contact
Credit Research Foundation
8840 Columbia 100 Parkway
Columbia, MD 21045-2158
Tel: 410-740-5499
http://www.crfonline.org

For information on certification, continuing education, and the banking and credit industry, contact
National Association of Credit Management
8840 Columbia 100 Parkway
Columbia, MD 21045-2158
Tel: 410-740-5560
http://www.nacm.org

Financial Analysts

OVERVIEW

Financial analysts, also called *security analysts* and *investment analysts,* analyze the financial situation of companies and recommend ways for these companies to manage, spend, and invest their money. The goal of financial analysts is to help their employer or clients make informed, lucrative financial decisions. They assemble and evaluate the company's financial data and assess investment opportunities. They look at the company's financial history, the direction that company wants to take in the future, the company's place in the industry, and current and projected economic conditions. Financial analysts also conduct similar research on companies that might become investment opportunities. They write reports and compile spreadsheets that show the benefits of certain investments or selling certain securities.

Among the businesses employing financial analysts are banks, brokerage firms, government agencies, mutual funds, and insurance and investment companies. There are approximately 250,600 financial analysts employed in the United States.

HISTORY

U.S. securities markets date back to the early years of the nation. The first U.S. stock exchanges were created in the 1790s. The New York Stock Exchange (which did not get its present name until 1863) was one of these. It started as a group of men who did their trading under a tree at 68 Wall Street. The markets grew as the country's industries developed. The unregulated U.S. securities markets flourished

School Subjects
Business
Computer science
Mathematics

Personal Skills
Communication/ideas
Leadership/management

Work Environment
Primarily indoors
Primarily one location

Minimum Education Level
Bachelor's degree

Salary Range
$44,080 to $73,670 to
$139,350+

Certification or Licensing
Recommended (certification)
Required for certain positions
(licensing)

Outlook
Much faster than the average

DOT
N/A

GOE
13.02.04

NOC
1112

O*NET-SOC
13–2051.00

just following World War I. According to the U.S. Securities and Exchange Commission (SEC), some 20 million people "took advantage of post-war prosperity and set out to make their fortunes in the stock market." The stock market crash of 1929, however, wiped out the savings of many investors. Consumers became wary of the markets and hesitated to invest again. Congress created the SEC in 1934 to keep watch over the markets and institute rules and regulations in the industry. The goal was to ensure that companies and stockbrokers divulged truthful information about their businesses, the investments offered, and the potential risk involved.

The Financial Analysts Federation (FAF), a group for investment professionals, was created in 1947. The FAF brought some prestige and respect to the profession. Then in 1959 the Institute of Chartered Financial Analysts (ICFA) was developed. Financial analysts who successfully completed the ICFA examination received the designation Chartered Financial Analyst (CFA). In June 1963, 268 analysts became the first group of CFA charterholders. The FAF and ICFA went on to merge in 1990, creating the Association for Investment Management and Research, which was renamed the CFA Institute in 2004.

Deregulation in the 1970s and 1980s brought about greater competition in the industry and more crossover between finance and banking. Knowledgeable professionals like financial analysts were in greater demand to help businesses keep up with the growing number and complexity of investment options. Financial analysts who forecast the rapid rise of technology stocks in the late 1990s were hailed in the industry and the media. But the steep decline of many of those same stocks by 2000–01 led to questions and concerns about the truthfulness of the information reported by certain financial analysts. In late 2000 the SEC instituted the Regulation Fair Disclosure rule, calling for fuller and more honest public disclosure of investment information. Public officials have continued to investigate and prosecute corruption and dishonesty on Wall Street.

Not only have technology stocks affected the business conducted by financial analysts, but so have changes in technology itself. Spreadsheet and statistical software programs afford financial analysts many improved and sophisticated options in compiling and presenting data. What in its early days was little more than deal making among a small group of men beneath a tree has evolved into a worldwide, high-tech, competitive industry, and financial analysts play an integral role in it.

The job of financial analyst continues to evolve. Skilled, honest financial analysts will remain in demand because of the increasingly complex nature of investing.

THE JOB

The specific types, direction, and scope of analyses performed by financial analysts are many and varied, depending on the industry, the employer or client, and the analyst's training and years of experience, but there are two main types of analysts: *buy-side analysts* and *sell-side analysts*. Buy-side analysts conduct research to track down desirable investments, usually for money management firms (e.g., mutual, hedge, or pension funds; insurance companies; and nonprofit organizations with large endowments). The research is used solely for the firm's purposes in the hopes of turning a profit after purchase. If the firm makes money from the buy-side analyst's investment recommendation, it's likely the analyst will be compensated. Sell-side analysts (also known as *sales analysts* or *Wall Street analysts*) similarly conduct research to track down desirable investments, but do so for brokerage firms. These investment recommendations ("buy," "sell," or "hold") are passed on to a firm's clients and also the public. The firm makes a commission based on customer orders rather than investment performance. The more orders that come in, the more money the firm is likely to pay the analyst.

Financial analysts study their employer's or client's financial status and make financial and investment recommendations. To arrive at these recommendations, financial analysts examine the employer's or client's financial history and objectives, income and expenditures, risk tolerance, and current investments. Once they understand the employer's or client's financial standing and investment goals, financial analysts scout out potential investment opportunities. They research other companies, perhaps in a single industry, that their employer or client may want to invest in. This in-depth research consists of investigating the business of each company, including history, past and potential earnings, and products. Based on their findings, financial analysts may recommend that their employer or client buy stock in these companies. If the employer or client already holds stock in a particular company, financial analysts' research may indicate that stocks should be held or sold, or that more should be purchased.

Financial analysts work for companies in any number of industries, including banking, transportation, health care, technology, telecommunications, and energy. While investment options and concerns differ among these, financial analysts still apply the same basic analytic tools in devising investment strategies. They try to learn everything they can about the industry they are working in. They study the markets and make industry comparisons. They also research past performance and future trends of bonds and other investments.

Financial analysts compile many types of reports on their employer or client and on investment opportunities, such as profit-and-loss statements and quarterly outlook statements. They help to develop budgets, analyze and oversee cash flow, and perform cost-benefit analyses. They conduct risk analyses to determine what the employer or client can risk at a given time and/or in the future. Another responsibility is to ensure that their employer or client meets any relevant tax or regulatory requirements. Financial analysts compile their work using various software programs, often developing financial models, such as charts or graphs, to display their data.

Companies that want to go public (sell company shares to individual investors for the first time) often ask financial analysts to make projections of future earnings as well as presentations for potential investors. Financial analysts also make sure that all paperwork is in order and compliant with Securities and Exchange Commission rules and regulations.

Entry-level financial analysts, usually working under direct supervision, mainly conduct research and compile statistical data. After a few years of experience, they become more involved in presenting reports. While a financial analyst generally offers recommendations, a senior financial analyst often has the authority to actually decide purchases or sales. Senior financial analysts implement a company's business plan. In larger companies, they also assist different departments in conducting their own financial analyses and business planning. Those in senior positions become supervisors as well, training junior financial analysts.

Many specialties fall under the job title of financial analyst. These specialties vary from employer to employer, and duties overlap between different types of analysts. In smaller firms a financial analyst may have extensive responsibility, while at larger firms a financial analyst may specialize in one of any number of areas. *Budget analysts,* often *accountants* or *controllers,* look at the operating costs of a company or its individual departments and prepare budget reports. *Credit analysts* examine credit records to determine the potential risk in extending credit or lending money. *Investment analysts* evaluate investment data so they can make suitable investment recommendations. *Mergers and acquisitions analysts* conduct research and make recommendations relating to company mergers and acquisitions. *Money market analysts* assess financial data and investment opportunities, giving advice specifically in the area of money markets. *Ratings analysts* explore a company's financial situation to determine whether or not it will be able to repay debts. *Risk analysts* focus on evaluating the risks of investments. The intent is to identify and then minimize a company's risks and losses. *Security analysts* specialize in studying securities, such as stocks and bonds. *Tax analysts* prepare, file, and examine federal, state, and local tax payments and returns for their employer or client and perhaps also for local affiliates. They analyze tax issues and keep up with tax law changes. *Treasury analysts* manage their company's or client's daily cash position, prepare cash journal entries, initiate wire transfers, and perform bank reconciliations.

Personal financial advisers have many similar responsibilities (assessing finances, projecting income, recommending investments), but these are performed on behalf of individuals rather than companies. (For more information, see the article Financial Planners.)

REQUIREMENTS

High School

Since financial analysts work with numbers and compile data, you should take as many math classes as are available. Accounting, business, economics, and computer classes will be helpful as well. A good grasp of computer spreadsheet programs such as Excel is vital. Take extra care as you research and write reports in any subject matter or in public speaking, and it will pay off later when you must conduct investment research and write and present investment recommendations.

Postsecondary Training

Most employers require that financial analysts hold a bachelor's degree in accounting, business administration, economics, finance, or statistics. Other possible majors include communications, international business, and public administration. Some companies will hire you if you hold a bachelor's degree in another discipline as long as you can demonstrate mathematical ability. In college, take business, economics, and statistics courses. Since computer technology plays such a big role in a financial analyst's work, computer classes can be helpful as well. English composition classes can prepare you for the writing you will need to do when preparing reports. Some employers require a writing sample prior to an interview.

Financial analysts generally continue to take courses to keep up with the ongoing changes in the world of finance, including international trade, state and federal laws and regulations, and computer technology. Proficiency in certain databases, presentation graphics, spreadsheets, and other software is expected. Some employers require their employees to have a master's degree in business administration or finance.

Many top firms offer summer internship programs. Check company Web sites for the particulars, such as assignments and qualifications. An internship can provide you with helpful contacts and increase your chances of landing a job when you finish with college.

Certification or Licensing

Financial analysts can earn the title chartered financial analyst (CFA). While certification is not required, it is recommended. The CFA program, which is administered by the CFA Institute, consists of three levels of examinations. These rigorous exams deal with such topics as economics, financial statement analysis, corporate finance, and portfolio management. The CFA Institute states that a candidate may need to spend an average of 300 hours studying to prepare for each level. The Motley Fool, a financial education company (http://www.fool.com), reported that about 50 percent of the candidates fail the first level. A candidate can take only one level per year, so a minimum of three years is required to become a CFA charterholder. If a candidate fails a level, it can be taken the next year. Candidates who do not successfully complete all three levels within seven years must reregister.

Before taking the exams, you must already have a bachelor's degree (or four years of professional experience). There is no required course of study. Prior to earning the CFA charter, you must have spent three years in a related field working in the investment decision-making process and you must first apply to become a member of the CFA Institute as well as a local society.

The CFA charter is recognized around the world as a standard in the finance industry. Many employers expect job seekers to be CFA charterholders.

The Association for Financial Professionals and American Academy of Financial Management also offer certification.

For certain upper-level positions, some firms require that you have a certified public accountant license. Visit its Web site, http://www.afponline.org, for more information.

The Financial Industry Regulatory Authority is the primary licensing organization for the securities industry. Visit its Web site, http://www.finra.org, for more information on licensing requirements for financial analysts who work as financial services brokers.

Other Requirements

Research, organizational, and communication skills are crucial for this job. Financial analysts conduct in-depth research, often looking for hard-to-find data. Organizational skills are important when it comes to compiling and presenting this data. Once you have explored a company's financial situation, you must communicate complicated ideas through presentations and/or written reports. You should be able to clearly communicate ideas, both verbally when making presentations and on paper when writing reports.

The work requires strong analytic skills, so a knack for numbers and attention to detail are also helpful. An interest in solving problems will go a long way. It is important that a financial analyst be accurate and thorough in preparing financial statements.

You should enjoy reading and be able to retain what you read, since it is important to keep up with what's happening in the industry and take it into account when offering financial solutions to employers or clients. Since many financial analysts must travel at a moment's notice to conduct research or complete a deal, flexibility is another important characteristic.

Financial analysts should be able to work well under pressure, as this line of work often demands long hours and entails strict deadlines. You should have good interpersonal skills and enjoy interacting with others. Deals or important contacts can be made at social functions or business conferences.

EXPLORING

There are many sources of information dealing with the financial services industry. Read publications such as *Barron's* (http://online.barrons.com), *Wall Street Journal* (http://online.wsj.com), *Forbes* (http://www.forbes.com), *Bloomberg Businessweek* (http://www.businessweek.com), *Fortune* (http://money.cnn.com/magazines/fortune), and *Financial Times* (http://www.ft.com/home/uk). In either the print or online versions, you will find a wealth of information on stocks, mutual funds, finance, education, careers, salaries, global business, and more. You can also use these resources to conduct company research. You might have to become a subscriber to access certain sections online.

AnalystForum (http://www.analystforum.com) is a resource for chartered financial analysts and CFA candidates. While this site won't be of much use to you until you've launched your career, you can find links to financial, investment, and security analyst society sites. From within these societies, you can perhaps track down a professional who would be willing to do an information interview with you.

While in high school, you might volunteer to handle the bookkeeping for a school club or student government, or help balance the family checking account to become familiar with simple book-keeping practices. Your school may have an investment club you can join. If not, ask a parent or teacher to help you research and analyze investment opportunities. Choose a specific industry (e.g., telecommunications, technology, or health care), study companies in that industry, and select and track several stocks that appear to have growth potential.

EMPLOYERS

Approximately 250,600 financial analysts are employed in the United States. Financial analysts work in the public and private sectors. Employers include banks, brokerage and securities firms, corporations, government agencies, manufacturers, mutual and pension funds, and financial management, insurance, investment, trust, and utility companies. Many financial analysts are self-employed. According to the *Occupational Outlook Handbook,* about 47 percent of financial analysts work for security and commodity brokers, banks and credit institutions, and insurance carriers.

Since financial analysts often work in Wall Street companies, many employers are found in New York City. They are also concentrated in other large cities but work in smaller cities as well.

STARTING OUT

Representatives from hiring companies (e.g., banks, brokerage firms, or investment companies) may visit college campuses to meet with students interested in pursuing careers as financial analysts. College career services offices will have details on such visits. Company Web sites may also offer campus recruiting schedules.

Gaining an entry-level position can be difficult. Some companies offer in-house training, but many don't. Beginning as a research assistant might be one way to break into the business. Read member profiles at association sites to see where members have worked as financial analysts. Explore those companies that look appealing.

Make contacts and network with other financial analysts. Your local CFA Institute society or chapter will probably hold regular meetings, affording ample networking opportunities. You can become a CFA Institute member whether or not you are a CFA charterholder, but charterholders enjoy full member benefits, such as access to job postings. (Complete details, including listings for local societies and chapters, can be found at the CFA Institute Web site, https://www.cfainstitute.org.) Also, internships can be an excellent way to make contacts and gain experience in the field.

As an interview tool, the New York Society of Security Analysts suggests that you compile an investment recommendation for potential clients to give them an idea of the kind of research you're capable of and how you present your data.

You can search for job ads online. One resource is eFinancial-Careers (http://www.efinancialcareers.com). If you know what companies you'd like to work for, visit their Web sites. Chances are you will find online job listings there.

ADVANCEMENT

Financial analysts who accurately prepare their employer's or client's financial statements and who offer investment advice that results in profits will likely be rewarded for their efforts. Rewards come in the form of promotions and/or bonuses. Successful financial analysts may become senior financial analysts, sometimes in only three or four years. Some become portfolio or financial managers. Rather than simply making recommendations on their company's or client's investment policies, those who advance to a senior position have more decision-making responsibility.

Some financial analysts move on to jobs as investment bankers or advisers. Others become officers in various departments in their company. Positions include chief financial officer and vice president of finance. In time, some cultivate enough contacts to be able to start their own consulting firms.

EARNINGS

The U.S. Department of Labor, reports that median annual earnings of financial analysts were $73,670 in 2009. Top earners (the top 10 percent) made more than $139,350, and the lowest salaries (the lowest 10 percent) were less than $44,080. If the investments of financial analysts' employers or clients perform well, it is not uncommon for those financial analysts to receive a bonus in addition to their salary. With bonuses, skilled financial analysts can make much more than their base salary.

Benefits include paid vacation, health, disability, life insurance, and retirement or pension plans. Some employers also offer profit-sharing plans. Tuition reimbursement may also be available.

WORK ENVIRONMENT

Most financial analysts work in an office in a corporate setting. Frequently, they work alone (e.g., when conducting research or talking on the phone to clients). Some may work out of their homes. Much time is spent working on a computer, doing research and compiling data. Travel is frequently required—there are meetings and social functions to attend, clients to meet, and companies to research at their place of business. Because financial analysts spend much of their normal business hours talking or meeting with clients, they often conduct research after hours and generally work long days. It is not uncommon for financial analysts to clock well in excess of 50 hours per week.

OUTLOOK

The state of the economy and the stock market has a direct effect on the employment outlook for financial analysts. When the economy is doing well, companies are more likely to make investments, resulting in a need for financial analysts. When the economy is doing poorly, companies are less likely to make investments, and there will be less need for financial analysts. The *Occupational Outlook Handbook* (*OOH*), anticipating an increase in business investments, predicts that employment for financial analysts will grow much faster than the average for all careers through 2018. The *OOH* notes, too, that international securities markets, the complexity of financial products, and business mergers and acquisitions demand financial analysts to sort through all the issues involved. Because of the close scrutiny analysts have been under, it might become more desirable for financial analysts to hold the CFA charter. Despite the prediction for excellent growth, competition for positions as financial analysts will be very strong since many people are interested in entering the field. Applicants with strong college grades in finance, accounting, and economics courses, a graduate degree in business or finance, and certification will have the best job prospects.

Individual investing will also affect the need for financial analysts, in that the more people invest in mutual funds [often through 401(k) plans], the greater the need there will be for financial analysts to recommend financial products to the mutual fund companies.

FOR MORE INFORMATION

For information on certification, contact
American Academy of Financial Management
http://www.aafm.us

This organization's Web site offers industry news and certification information.

Association for Financial Professionals
4520 East West Highway, Suite 750
Bethesda, MD 20814-3574
Tel: 301-907-2862
http://www.afponline.org

*For complete CFA Institute information, including lists of institute
societies, publications, news, conference details, and certification
information, contact*
CFA Institute
560 Ray C. Hunt Drive
Charlottesville, VA 22903-2981
Tel: 800-247-8132
E-mail: info@cfainstitute.org
http://www.cfainstitute.org

*Visit the NYSSA Web site for information on membership for col-
lege students, a list of top employers of financial analysts, and scholarships for graduate students.*
New York Society of Security Analysts (NYSSA)
1540 Broadway, Suite 1010
New York, NY 10036-2714
Tel: 212-541-4530
http://www.nyssa.org

*For information on laws and regulations pertaining to investors and
the securities markets, contact*
U.S. Securities and Exchange Commission
Office of Investor Education and Advocacy
100 F Street, NE
Washington, DC 20549-2000
Tel: 202-942-8088
E-mail: publicinfo@sec.gov
http://www.sec.gov

*This Web site has links to financial, investment, and security analyst
societies.*
AnalystForum
http://www.analystforum.com

For issues of interest to senior finance executives, see
CFO.com
http://www.cfo.com

INTERVIEW

Victor Jarosiewicz, ASA, CFA, is a financial analyst at PCE Valuations, LLC. He discussed his career with the editors of Careers in Focus: Financial Services.

Q. Why did you decide to pursue a career as a financial analyst?

A. I always knew I was better at solving problems than rolling up my sleeves, and that I would like applying myself in a professional environment more than in a technical or vocational field. While I can do physical work and I am pretty good at fixing things, really, once I saw Michael J. Fox in the movie *Secret of My Success* I knew I'd want to be in investment banking or in a related field.

I'm good at math, I'm good at writing, I'm good at understanding how businesses make money (it's not as easy as it seems), but I didn't want just to buy a business or start one on my own. I have found that as a financial analyst I get to use all my skills to look at how other people run their businesses and I make financial judgments of how well they do, and I help businesses and their owners make (hopefully) better financial decisions.

Q. Can you take us through a day in your work life?

A. The work of a financial analyst in a corporation is quite different from that of an investment banking analyst, and again different from a stock or portfolio analyst. In my niche within investment banking and business valuations, work is geared to helping owners sell their companies or determine the value of shares and investments. There are always deadlines and client expectations and multiple projects to work on at any one time. On any given day, the work includes researching public companies and acquisitions of companies, analyzing the impact of industry conditions and a firm's profitability on their value, and determining a reasonable range of value either as an asking price to sell a company or as the reported conclusion that others, such as certified public accountants and investors, will rely on to make decisions.

An analyst is responsible for all aspects of a project—from initial research, to spreadsheet model creation, to analysis and conclusions, to the writing of the report. As his or her experience grows, he or she becomes more responsible for interacting with clients, the senior management of companies, and other professional firms. Ultimately, the analysts transition into a more senior role, supervising and reviewing the work of more junior analysts, and at the same time expanding their duties to include business development and sales efforts, whether by supporting sales teams or by making appointments and holding meetings with prospective clients on their own.

Hours can vary greatly, but generally the more successful a firm and analyst, the more hours need to be invested to advance in one's career. This is not a career choice for slackers. Investment banking has had a reputation for demanding schedules, with some Wall Street analysts working more than 80 hours a week regularly for the first several years of their career. However, virtually all financial analyst roles are salaried professional jobs, where the expectation is to put in however many hours are required to provide the deliverables that are expected by clients and supervisors. Just as important as the willingness to work the hours required is the ability to work and learn independently, as successful firms are very busy and much of the training is on the job—sort of a professional apprenticeship, one might say.

Q. What do you like least and most about being a financial analyst?

A. I like most the interaction my work gives me with business leaders across all sorts of industries, and the ability to make a difference in their lives. The least favorite part of being a financial analyst is that it can become a little removed and have a bit of the "ivory tower" feel to it from time to time. However, getting out and meeting with clients, business owners, other professionals, and even volunteering in organizations apart from work, makes things balance out.

Q. What are the most important personal and professional skills for financial analysts?

A. The ability to communicate key issues, decision points, and solutions—whether in presentations, in writing, or in person—is paramount. The softer skill of working well on a team is essential to a productive and successful career. We expect all the candidates we interview to have very good math and spreadsheet model building skills, but the ones that stand out are those who will be team players and those who can convey their ideas quickly and convincingly.

Q. What is one of the most interesting or rewarding things that has happened to you while working in the field?

A. I have had the opportunity to meet and get to know some of the leading experts from all over the world in my field and in finance. More importantly, I have been able to help business owners make decisions that positively affected hundreds of millions of dollars of investments and hundreds of employees and families.

Q. What is the employment outlook for financial analysts?

A. Times are tough now, particularly for analyst positions, but that all depends on the industry or niche. Right now, defense and health care are sectors in demand and growing, and corporate financial analyst positions there are being sought after. However, as capital markets rebound, investment banks and wealth management companies will hire analysts as their business grows. As the economy begins to expand again, and more growth opportunities are created, all types of corporations will add analysts to help sort through those opportunities. For high school students, long-term prospects for financial analyst careers are very good; it is often a path that leads to managing large companies or large amounts of capital, and having a profound impact on their communities and the economy.

Financial Institution Officers and Managers

OVERVIEW

Financial institution officers and managers oversee the activities of banks and personal credit institutions such as credit unions and finance companies. These establishments serve business, government, and individuals. They lend money, maintain savings, enable people and businesses to write checks or make online payments for goods and services, rent safe-deposit boxes for storing valuables, manage trust funds, advise clients on investments and business affairs, issue credit cards and traveler's checks, and take payments for gas and electric bills. There are approximately 539,300 financial managers (including those working outside of financial institutions) employed in the United States.

HISTORY

The modern concept of bank notes, or currency, developed in the 17th century. Goldsmiths in London began to issue paper receipts for gold and other valuables that were deposited in their warehouses. The paper money we use today is a modern version of these 17th-century receipts.

The first bank in the United States, Bank of North America, was chartered by the Continental Congress in 1781. By the early 1900s, banks had become so numerous that federal control of banks was needed. The Federal Deposit System, as we know it today, is the result of the efforts to coordinate the activities of the many banks throughout the nation. As banks grew in number and competed to attract new customers, financial professionals developed a variety of new services for banks to offer. Advancements in technology made many of these new services possible and, often, changed the way people thought about money. For example, banks introduced the first credit cards that were accepted by multiple vendors (cards that we know as Visa, MasterCard, etc.) in the late 1950s and 1960s. The introduction of these credit cards was made possible by bank computers that were able to track transactions and signal when spending limits were reached. Today, credit cards have become so commonplace that CardWeb.com estimates that there are approximately 6,000 credit card issuers. The average American has eight credit cards. The average credit card debt per household is $7,394, according to IndexCreditCards.com.

The banking industry continues to use technology to expand its services. Today, most major banks offer online banking. Other smaller banks at least have a presence on the Web. It is estimated

Fun Facts About Coins

- The United States Mint, which produces the coins we use every day, was created by an act of Congress on April 2, 1792.
- The first mint buildings were constructed in Philadelphia, the nation's capital at the time. The Philadelphia Mint is still in operation today. Along with the Denver Mint (established in 1862), it minted more than 6.2 billion coins in 2010.
- The first coins ever produced by the United States Mint: 11,178 copper cents, which were delivered in March 1793.
- Until 1837, pennies were made of pure copper. Today, pennies are made up of 97.5 percent zinc and 2.5 percent copper (copper-plated zinc).
- To conserve copper during World War II, the United States Mint issued "gray" steel pennies.
- Only two women have ever been portrayed on circulating coins in the United States. Sacagawea—a Shoshone woman who played a key role in guiding the explorers Lewis and Clark across what is now the western United States—appeared on the dollar coin, which was introduced in 2000 and is still in circulation today. Susan B. Anthony, a women's suffragist, appeared on the dollar coin, which was circulated from 1979 to 1981.

Source: The United States Mint

that more than 55 million Americans bank online, and this number is expected to increase in the future.

Within the past 25 years, the number of banks and other financial institutions—as well as banking options—have grown extensively, and many financial professionals are needed to help run the banking industry.

THE JOB

Financial institutions include commercial banks, which provide full banking service for business, government, and individuals; investment banks, which offer their clients financial counseling and brokering; Federal Reserve Banks, whose customers are affiliated banks in their districts; or other organizations such as credit unions and finance companies.

These institutions employ many officers and managers whose duties vary depending on the type and size of the firm as well as on their own area of responsibility. All financial institutions operate under the direction of a president, who is guided by policies set by the board of directors. Vice presidents are department heads who are sometimes also responsible for certain key clients. Controllers handle bank funds, properties, and equipment. Large institutions may also have treasurers, loan officers, and officers in charge of departments such as trust, credit, and investment. A number of these positions are described in more detail in the following paragraphs.

The *financial institution president* directs the overall activities of the bank or consumer credit organization, making sure that its objectives are achieved without violating government regulations or overlooking any legal requirements. The officers are responsible for earning as much of a return as possible on the institution's investments within the restrictions demanded by government and sound business practices. They help set policies pertaining to investments, loans, interest, and reserves. They coordinate the activities of the various divisions and delegate authority to subordinate officers, who administer the operation of their own areas of responsibility. Financial institution presidents study financial reports and other data to keep up with changes in the economy that may affect their firm's policies.

The *vice president* coordinates many of the operations of the institution. This person is responsible for the activities of a regional bank office, branch bank, and often an administrative bank division or department. As designated by the board of directors, the vice president supervises programs such as installment loan, foreign trade, customer service, trust, and investment. The vice president also prepares studies for management and planning, like workload and budget estimates and activity and analysis reports.

The *administrative secretary* usually writes directions for supervisory workers that outline and explain policy. The administrative secretary acts, in effect, as an intermediary between minor supervisory workers and the executive officers.

The *financial institution treasurer* directs the bank's monetary programs, transactions, and security measures in accordance with banking principles and legislation. Treasurers coordinate program activity and evaluate operating practices to ensure efficient operations. They oversee receipt, disbursement, and expenditure of money, and sign documents approving or affecting monetary transactions. They direct the safekeeping and control of assets and securities and maintain specified legal cash reserves. They review financial and operating statements and present reports and recommendations to bank officials or board committees.

Controllers authorize the use of funds kept by the treasurer. They also supervise the maintenance of accounts and records, and analyze these records so that the directors or other bank officials will know how much the bank is spending for salaries, operating expenses, and other expenses. Controllers often formulate financial policies.

The *financial institution manager* establishes and maintains relationships with the community. This person's responsibility is to supervise accounting and reporting functions and to establish operating policies and procedures. The manager directs several activities within the bank. The assets, records, collateral, and securities held by the financial institution are in the manager's custody. Managers approve loans of various types, such as credit, commercial, real estate, and consumer loans. They also direct personnel in trust activities.

The *loan officer* and the *credit and collection manager* both deal with customers who are seeking or have obtained loans or credit. The loan officer specializes in examining and evaluating applications for lines of credit, installment credit, or commercial, real estate, and consumer loans and has the authority to approve them within a specified limit or recommend their approval to the loan committee. To determine the feasibility of granting a loan request, the officer analyzes the applicant's financial status, credit, and property evaluation. The job may also include handling foreclosure proceedings. Depending on training and experience, officers may analyze potential loan markets to develop prospects for loans. They negotiate the terms of transaction and draw up the requisite documents to buy and sell contracts, loans, or real estate. Credit and collection managers make up collection notices for customers who already have credit. When the bank has difficulty collecting accounts or receives a worthless check, credit and collection managers take steps to correct the situation. Managers must keep records of all credit and collection transactions.

Loan counselors study the records of the account when payments on a loan are overdue and contact the borrower to discuss payment of the loan. They may analyze the borrower's financial problems and make new arrangements for repayment of the loan. If a loan account is uncollectible, they prepare a report for the bank or institution's files.

Credit card operations managers are responsible for the overall credit card policies and operations of a bank, commercial establishment, or credit card company. They establish procedures for verifying the information on application forms, determine applicants' credit worthiness, approve the issuance of credit cards, and set a credit limit on each account. These managers coordinate the work involved with reviewing unpaid balances, collecting delinquent accounts, investigating and preventing fraud, voiding lost or stolen credit cards, keeping records, and exchanging information with the company's branches and other credit card companies.

The *letter of credit negotiator* works with clients who hold letters of credit used in international banking. This person contacts foreign banks, suppliers, and other sources to obtain documents needed to authorize the requested loan. Then the negotiator checks to see if the documents have been completed correctly so that the conditions set forth in the letter of credit meet with policy and code requirements. Before authorizing payment, the negotiator verifies the client's credit rating and may request increasing the collateral or reducing the amount of purchases, amending the contract accordingly. The letter of credit negotiator specifies the method of payment and informs the foreign bank when a loan has gone unpaid for a certain length of time.

The *trust officer* directs operations concerning the administration of private, corporate, and probate trusts. Officers examine or draft trust agreements to ensure compliance with legal requirements and terms creating trusts. They locate, inventory, and evaluate assets of probated accounts. They also direct realization of assets, liquidation of liabilities, payment of bills, preparation of federal and state tax returns on trust income, and collection of earnings. They represent the institution in trust fund negotiations.

Reserve officers maintain the institution's reserve funds according to policy and as required by law. They regulate the flow of money through branches, correspondent banks, and the Federal Reserve Bank. They also consolidate financial statements, calculate the legal reserve, and compile statistical and analytical reports of the reserves.

Foreign-exchange traders maintain the balance that the institution has on deposit in foreign banks to ensure its foreign-exchange position and determine the prices at which that exchange will be purchased and sold. Their conclusions are based on an analysis of demand, supply, and the stability of the currency. They establish local rates of exchange based upon money market quotations or the customer's financial standing. They also buy and sell foreign-exchange drafts and compute the proceeds.

The *securities trader* performs securities investment and counseling service for the bank and its customers. They study financial background and future trends and advise financial institution officers and customers regarding investments in stocks and bonds. They transmit buy-and-sell orders to a trading desk or broker as directed and recommend purchase, retention, or sale of issues. They compute extensions, commissions, and other charges for billing customers and making payments for securities.

The *operations officer* is in charge of the internal operations in a department or branch office of a financial institution. This person is responsible for the smooth and efficient operation of a particular area. Duties include interviewing, hiring, and directing the training of employees, as well as supervising their activities, evaluating their performance, and making certain that they comply with established procedures. Operations officers audit accounts, records, and certifications and verify the count of incoming cash. They prepare reports on the activities of the department or branch, control the supply of money for its needs, and perform other managerial tasks of a general nature.

The *credit union manager* directs the operations of credit unions, which are chartered by the state or federal government to provide savings and loan services to their members. This manager reviews loan applications, arranges automatic payroll deductions for credit union members wishing to make regular savings deposits or loan payments, and assists in collecting delinquent accounts. Managers prepare financial statements, help the government audit credit union records, and supervise bookkeeping and clerical activities. Acting as management representative of the credit union, credit union managers have the power to sign legal documents and checks on behalf of the board of directors. They also oversee control of the credit union's assets and advise the board on how to invest its funds.

REQUIREMENTS

High School

You will need at least a bachelor's degree if you want to work as a financial institution officer or manager. While you are in high school, therefore, you should take classes that will give you a solid preparation for college. Such classes include mathematics, such as algebra and geometry, science, history, and a foreign language. Take English courses to improve your researching, writing, and communication skills. Also, take computer classes. Computer technology is an integral part of today's financial world, and you will benefit from being familiar with this tool. Finally, if your high school offers classes in economics, accounting, or finance, be sure to take these courses. The course work will not only give you an opportunity to gain knowledge but will also allow you to see if you enjoy working with numbers and theories.

Postsecondary Training

Suggested college majors include accounting, economics, finance, or business administration with an emphasis on accounting or finance. You will need to continue honing your computer skills during this time. Also, you should take business law classes. Federal and state laws regarding business and finance change, so you will need to familiarize yourself with current regulations.

Financial institutions increasingly seek candidates with master's degrees in business administration for positions as managers. So keep in mind that you may have to pursue further education even after you have completed your bachelor's degree. No matter what level of degree you obtain, however, you will also need to keep up your education even as you work. Many financial management and banking associations offer continuing education programs in conjunction with colleges or universities. These programs are geared toward advancing and updating your knowledge of subjects such as changing banking regulations, financial analysis, and international banking.

Certification or Licensing

Certification is one way to show your commitment to the field, improve your skills, and increase your possibilities for advancement. Professional certification is available in specialized fields such as investment and credit management. Requirements for earning the designation chartered financial analyst, which is conferred by the CFA Institute, include having the educational background to be able to do master's level work, passing three levels of tests, and having three or more years of experience in the field. The National Association of Credit Management offers business credit professionals a three-part certification program that consists of work experience and examinations. Financial managers pass through the level of credit business associate to credit business fellow to certified credit executive. The Association for Financial Professionals confers the certified treasury professional (formerly known as the certified cash manager) and the certified treasury professional associate designations. Applicants must pass an examination and have working experience in the field. The American Academy of Financial Management offers a variety of certification designations. Visit its Web site, http:// www.aafm.us, for a complete list and requirements.

Other Requirements

In the banking business, the ability to get along well with others is essential. You should be able to show tact and convey a feeling of understanding and confidence. Honesty is perhaps the most important qualification for this job. These officers and managers handle large sums of money and have access to confidential financial information about the individuals and business concerns associated with their institutions. Therefore, if you are interested in this career, you must have a high degree of personal integrity. Other key traits include strong organizational, problem-solving, and leadership skills.

EXPLORING

Except for high school courses that are business oriented, you will find few opportunities for experience and exploration during high school. Ask your teacher or counselor to arrange a class tour of a financial institution. This will at least give you a taste of how banking services work. You can gain the most valuable experience by finding a part-time or a summer job in a bank or other institution that sometimes hires qualified high school or college students. Finally, to gain some hands-on experience with managing money, consider joining a school or local club in which you could work as the treasurer.

EMPLOYERS

Financial managers and related workers hold approximately 539,300 jobs. They primarily work for commercial banks, credit unions, savings and loan associations, and mortgage and finance companies.

STARTING OUT

One way to enter banking as a regular employee is through part-time or summer employment. Anyone can apply for a position by writing to a financial institution officer in charge of personnel or by arranging for an interview. Many institutions advertise in the classified section of local newspapers. The larger banks recruit on college campuses. An officer will visit a campus and conduct interviews at that time. Student career services offices can also arrange interviews.

ADVANCEMENT

There is no one method for advancement among financial institution officers. Advancement depends on the size of the institution, the services it offers, and the qualifications of the employee. Usually, it takes longer to advance working for smaller employers.

Financial institutions often offer special training programs that take place at night, during the summer, and in some special instances during scheduled working hours. People who take advantage of these opportunities usually find that advancement comes more quickly. The American Banking Institute (part of the American Bankers Association), for example, offers training in every phase of banking through its own facilities or the facilities of the local universities and banking organizations. The length of this training may vary from six months to two years. Years of service and experience are required for a top-level financial institution officer to become acquainted with policy, operations, customers, and the community. Similarly, the National Association of Credit Management offers training and instruction.

EARNINGS

Those who enter banking in the next few years will find their earnings to be dependent on their experience, the size of the institution, and its location. In general, starting salaries in financial institutions are not usually the highest, although among larger financial institutions in big cities, starting salaries often compare favorably with salaries in large corporations. After five to 10 years' experience, the salaries of officers usually are slightly higher than those in large corporations for people of comparable experience.

Financial managers earned a median annual salary of $101,190 in 2009, according to the U.S. Department of Labor (DOL). The lowest paid 10 percent of financial managers made less than $54,760, while the highest paid 25 percent earned $138,010 or more. Group life insurance, paid vacations, profit-sharing plans, and health care and retirement plans are some of the benefits offered to financial officers and managers.

WORK ENVIRONMENT

Working conditions in financial institutions are generally pleasant. They are usually clean, well maintained, and often air-conditioned. They are generally located throughout cities for the convenience of both customers and employees. Working hours for financial institution officers and managers may be somewhat irregular, as many organizations have expanded their hours of business.

OUTLOOK

Employment for financial institution officers and managers is expected to increase about as fast as the average for all occupations through 2018, according to the DOL. The need for skilled professionals will increase primarily as a result of greater domestic and foreign competition, changing laws affecting taxes and other financial matters, and a growing emphasis on accurate reporting of financial data for both financial institutions and corporations.

Competition for these jobs will be strong, however, for several reasons. Financial institution officers and managers are often promoted from within the ranks of the organization, and, once established in their jobs, they tend to stay for many years. Also, more qualified applicants are becoming available each year to fill vacancies; workers who have earned a master's degree in business administration and who are certified will enjoy the lowest unemployment rates. Chances for employment will be best for workers who are familiar with a range of financial services, such as banking, insurance, real estate, and securities, and for those experienced in computers and data processing systems.

FOR MORE INFORMATION

For information on certification, contact
American Academy of Financial Management
http://www.aafm.us

This organization has information about the banking industry and continuing education available through the American Institute of

Banking. It also has information on the Stonier National Graduate School of Banking.

American Bankers Association
1120 Connecticut Avenue, NW
Washington, DC 20036-3902
Tel: 800-226-5377
http://www.aba.com

For certification, industry news, and career information, contact
Association for Financial Professionals
4520 East West Highway, Suite 750
Bethesda, MD 20814-3574
Tel: 301-907-2862
http://www.afponline.org

For information on the chartered financial analyst designation, contact
CFA Institute
560 Ray C. Hunt Drive
Charlottesville, VA 22903-2981
Tel: 800-247-8132
E-mail: info@cfainstitute.org
https://www.cfainstitute.org

For information on mortgage banking, contact
Mortgage Bankers Association
1717 Rhode Island Avenue, NW, Suite 400
Washington, DC 20036-3023
Tel: 202-557-2700
http://www.mbaa.org

For information on certification, continuing education, and the banking and credit industry, contact
National Association of Credit Management
8840 Columbia 100 Parkway
Columbia, MD 21045-2158
Tel: 410-740-5560
http://www.nacm.org

Financial Institution Tellers, Clerks, and Related Workers

OVERVIEW

Financial institution tellers, clerks, and related workers perform many tasks in banks and other savings institutions. Tellers work at teller windows where they receive and pay out money, record customer transactions, cash checks, sell traveler's checks, and perform other banking duties. The most familiar teller is the *commercial teller,* who works with customers, handling check cashing, deposits, and withdrawals. Specialized tellers are also employed, especially at large financial institutions. Clerks' and related workers' jobs usually vary with the size of the institution. In small banks, a clerk or related worker may perform a combination of tasks, while in larger banks an employee may be assigned to one specialized duty. All banking activities are concerned with the safekeeping, exchange, record keeping, credit, and other uses of money. There are approximately 600,500 tellers employed in the United States.

HISTORY

The profession of banking is nearly as old as civilization itself. Ancient records show that the Babylonians, for example, had a fairly complex system of lending, borrowing, and depositing money even before 2500 B.C. Other early literature makes reference to "money-lenders" and "money-changers" as ancient writers, and travelers describe how they bought money in other countries by trading coins from their own homelands.

The term "bank" is derived from the Italian *banco,* meaning bench. Since the times of the Roman Empire, Italy has been an important trading and shipping nation. In medieval times, bankers set up benches on the streets and from these conducted their business of trading currencies and accepting precious metals and jewels for safekeeping. They also lent money at interest to finance the new ventures of shipping merchants and other businesses. Italian cities eventually established permanent banks, and this practice gradually spread north throughout Europe. During the 17th century important banking developments took place in England, which by that time had become a major trading nation. In 1694, the Bank of England was founded in London.

In the newly founded United States, the Continental Congress chartered the Bank of North America on December 31, 1781 in Philadelphia. The first state bank was chartered in Boston in 1784 as the Bank of Massachusetts. Although the development of banking in the United States has experienced periods of slow growth, political controversies, and numerous failures throughout history, Congress and the federal government have done a great deal to make the nation's banking system safer and more effective.

A high school senior in a job-training program learns how to conduct bank transactions. *(Aaron Flaum, AP Photo/NorwichBulletin.com)*

Today, banking, like many other professions, has turned to the use of automation, mechanization, computers, telecommunications, and many modern methods of bookkeeping and record systems. Banks and savings institutions employ thousands of workers so that they can offer all the modern banking conveniences that Americans enjoy today.

THE JOB

Several different types of tellers may work at a financial institution, depending on its size. The teller the average bank customer has the most contact with, however, is the commercial teller, also known as a *paying and receiving teller.* These tellers service the public directly by accepting customers' deposits and providing them with receipts, paying out withdrawals and recording the transactions, cashing checks, exchanging money for customers to provide them with certain kinds of change or currency, and accepting savings account deposits. At the beginning of the workday, each teller is given a cash drawer containing a certain amount of cash from the vault. During the day, this is the money they use for transactions with customers. Their work with the money and their record keeping must be accurate. At the end of their shifts, the tellers' cash drawers are recounted, and the amount must match up with the transactions done that day. A teller who has problems balancing his or her drawer will not be employed for very long.

Head tellers and *teller supervisors* train tellers, arrange work schedules, and monitor the tellers' records of the day's transactions. If there are any problems in balancing the cash drawers, the head teller or supervisor must try to figure out where the error occurred and reconcile the differences.

At large financial institutions, tellers may perform specialized duties and are identified by the transactions they handle. *Note tellers,* for example, are responsible for receiving and issuing receipts or payments on promissory notes and recording these transactions correctly. *Discount tellers* are responsible for issuing and collecting customers' notes. *Foreign banknote tellers* work in the exchange department, where they buy and sell foreign currency. When customers need to trade their foreign currency for U.S. currency, these tellers determine the current value of the foreign currency in dollars, count out the bills requested by the customer, and make change. These tellers may also sell foreign currency and traveler's checks for people traveling out of the country. *Collection and exchange tellers* accept payments in forms other than cash—contracts, mortgages, and bonds, for example.

While tellers' work involves much interaction with the public, most of the work done by clerks and other related workers is completed behind the scenes. Clerks and related workers are responsible for keeping depositors' money safe, the bank's investments healthy, and government regulations satisfied. All such workers assist in processing the vast amounts of paperwork that a bank generates. This paperwork may consist of deposit slips, checks, financial statements to customers, correspondence, record transactions, and reports for internal and external use. Depending on their job responsibilities, clerks may prepare, collect, send, index, or file these documents, as well as manage data and records created as a result of electronic transactions. In addition, they may talk with customers and other banks, take telephone calls, respond to e-mails, and perform other general office duties.

The tasks clerks and related workers perform also depend on the size of the financial institution. Duties may be more generalized in smaller facilities and very specialized at larger institutions. The nature of the bank's business and the array of services it offers may also determine a clerk's duties. Services may differ somewhat in a commercial bank from those in a savings bank, trust company, credit union, or savings and loans. In the past, banks generally lent money to businesses while savings and loan and credit unions lent to individuals, but these differences are disappearing over time.

Collection clerks process checks, coupons, and drafts that customers present to the financial institution for special handling. *Commodity-loan clerks* keep track of commodities (usually farm products) used as collateral by the foreign departments of large banks.

Banks employ *bookkeepers* to keep track of countless types of financial and administrative information. *Bookkeeping clerks* file checks, alphabetize paperwork to assist senior bookkeepers, and sort and list various other kinds of material.

Proof machine operators handle a machine that, in one single operation, can sort checks and other papers, add their amounts, and record totals. *Transit clerks* sort and list checks and drafts on other banks and prepare them for mailing or electronic transmission to those banks. *Statement clerks* send customers their account statements listing the withdrawals and deposits they have made. *Bookkeeping machine operators* maintain records of the various deposits, checks, and other items that are credited to or charged against customer accounts. Often they cancel checks and file them, provide customers with information about account balances, and prepare customers' statements for mailing.

Messengers deliver checks, drafts, letters, and other business papers to other financial institutions, business firms, and local and federal government agencies. Messengers who work only within the bank are often known as *pages*. *Trust-mail clerks* keep track of mail in trust departments.

Other clerks—*collateral-and-safekeeping clerks, reserves clerks,* and *interest clerks*—collect and record information about collateral, reserves, and interest rates and payments. *Letter-of-credit clerks* keep track of letters of credit for export and import purposes. *Wire-transfer clerks* direct the transfer of funds from one account to another.

In addition to working in banks, people employed by financial institutions may work at savings and loan associations, personal finance companies, credit unions, government agencies, and large businesses operating credit offices. Although tellers, clerks, and other workers' duties may differ among institutions, the needs for accuracy and honesty are the same. Financial institutions are usually pleasant, quiet places to work and have very up-to-date equipment and business machines. People who work in banking should be of good character and enjoy precision and detailed work.

REQUIREMENTS

High School

Most banks today prefer to hire individuals who have completed high school. If you take courses in bookkeeping, mathematics, business arithmetic, and business machines while in high school, you may have an advantage when applying for a job. Many banks now use computers to perform the routine tasks that workers formerly did by hand, so be sure to take computer science courses. Take English, speech, and foreign language classes to improve your communication skills, which you will need when interacting with customers and other workers. Some banks are interested in hiring college graduates (or those who have completed at least two years of college training) who can eventually move into managerial positions. Exchange clerks may be expected to know foreign languages. Additionally, some banks hire tellers who are proficient in one or more foreign languages to assist customers who do not speak English.

Postsecondary Training

Once hired, tellers, clerks, and related workers typically receive on-the-job training. At large institutions, tellers usually receive about one week of classroom training and then undergo on-the-job training for several weeks before they are allowed to work independently. Smaller financial institutions may only provide the on-the-job training in which new tellers are supervised in their work by experienced employees. Clerks may also need to undergo classroom instruction; for example, a bookkeeping clerk may need to take a class covering a certain computer program.

To enhance your possibility of getting a job as well as increase your skills, you may want to take business-related courses or courses for those in the financial industry at a local community college. Courses that may be helpful to take include records management, office systems and procedures, and computer database programming. Those with the most skills and training will find they usually have the best possibilities for advancing.

Numerous educational opportunities will be available to you once you have begun working—and gaining experience—in the financial world. For example, the American Institute of Banking (the educational division of the American Bankers Association)—has a vast array of adult education classes in business fields and offers training courses in numerous parts of the country that enable people to earn standard or graduate certificates in bank training. Individuals may also enroll in correspondence study courses.

Other Requirements

Because the work involves many details, a prime requirement for all bank employees is accuracy. Even the slightest error can cause untold extra hours of work and inconvenience or even monetary loss. A pleasing and congenial personality and the ability to get along well with fellow workers and the public are also necessary in this employment.

The physical requirements of the work are not very demanding, although many of these workers spend much of the day standing, which can be tiring. While working in this field, you will be expected to be neat, clean, and appropriately dressed for business.

Banks occasionally require lie detector tests of applicants, as well as fingerprint and background investigations if the job requires handling currency and finances. Those employees handling money or having access to confidential financial information may have to qualify for a personal bond. Some banks now require pre-employment drug testing, and random testing for drugs while under employment is becoming more typical.

Although integrity and honesty are important traits for an employee in any type of work, they are absolutely necessary if you hope to be employed in banks and other financial institutions where large sums of money are handled every day. Workers must also exhibit sound judgment and intelligence.

EXPLORING

You can explore the jobs in this field by visiting local financial institutions and talking with the directors of personnel or with people who work in these jobs. You should also consider serving as treasurer for your student government or a club that you are interested in. This will give you experience working with numbers and handling finances, as well as the opportunity to demonstrate responsibility. Learn about finances and the different kinds of financial instruments available by reading publications such as the business section of your local paper and *Money* magazine (also online at http://money.cnn.com).

Sometimes banks offer part-time employment to young people who feel they have a definite interest in pursuing a career in banking or those with business and clerical skills. Other types of part-time employment—where you learn basic business skills, how to interact with the public, and how to work well with other employees—may also be valuable training for those planning to enter these occupations.

EMPLOYERS

Approximately 600,500 tellers are employed in the United States; about 33 percent of them work part time. Financial institution tellers, clerks, and related workers are employed by commercial banks and other depository institutions and by mortgage banks and other nondepository institutions.

STARTING OUT

Private and state employment agencies frequently list available positions for financial institution tellers, clerks, and related workers. Newspaper help-wanted advertisements carry listings for such employees. Some large financial institutions visit schools and colleges to recruit qualified applicants to fill positions on their staff.

If you are interested in a job as a financial institution teller or clerk, try contacting the director of personnel at a bank or other institution to see if any positions are available. If any jobs are open, you may be asked to come in and fill out an application. It is very important, however, to arrange the appointment first by telephone or mail because drop-in visits are disruptive and seldom welcome.

If you know someone who is willing to give you a personal introduction to the director of personnel or to the officers of a bank, you may find that this will help you secure employment. Personal and business references can be important to bank employers when they hire new personnel.

Many financial institution clerks begin their employment as trainees in certain types of work, such as business machine operation or general or specialized clerical duties. Employees may start out as file clerks, transit clerks, or bookkeeping clerks and in some cases as pages or messengers. In general, beginning jobs are determined by the size of the institution and the nature of its operations. In banking work, employees are sometimes trained in related job tasks so that they might be promoted later.

ADVANCEMENT

Many banks and financial institutions follow a "promote-from-within" policy. Promotions are usually given on the basis of past job performance and consider the employee's seniority, ability, and general personal qualities. Clerks who have done well and established good reputations may be promoted to teller positions. Tellers, in turn, may be promoted to head teller or supervisory positions such as department head. Some head tellers may be transferred from their main branch bank to a smaller branch bank where they have greater responsibilities.

Employees who show initiative in their jobs and pursue additional education may advance into low-level officer positions, such as assistant trust officer. BAI and the American Institute of Banking (a division of the American Bankers Association) offer courses in various banking topics that can help employees learn new skills and prepare for promotions.

Advancement into the higher-level positions typically requires the employee to have a college or advanced degree.

EARNINGS

The earnings of financial institution workers vary by their specific duties, size and type of institution, and area of the country. According to the U.S. Department of Labor (DOL), full-time tellers earned a median annual income of $23,980 in 2009. Salaries ranged from less than $18,270 for the lowest paid 10 percent to more than $32,520 for the highest paid 10 percent.

The DOL also reports that bookkeeping, accounting, and auditing clerks earned a median full-time salary of $33,450 a year in 2009. The lowest paid 10 percent earned less than $21,280, and the highest paid 10 percent earned more than $50,450 a year. General office clerks employed in banks had median annual earnings of $26,541 in 2008.

Full-time financial institution tellers, clerks, and related workers may receive paid holidays and vacation days. Other benefits usually include group life and health insurance, hospitalization, and jointly financed retirement plans.

WORK ENVIRONMENT

Most financial institution professionals work a 40-hour week. Tellers may need to work irregular hours or overtime, since many banks stay open until 8:00 P.M. on Fridays and are open Saturday mornings to accommodate their customers. Bank clerks and accounting department employees may have to work overtime at least once a week and often at the close of each month's banking operations to process important paperwork. Check-processing workers who are employed in large financial institutions may work late evening or night shifts. Those employees engaged in computer operations may also work evening or night shifts because this equipment is usually run around the clock. Pay for overtime work is usually straight compensation.

Banks and other depository institutions are usually air-conditioned, pleasantly decorated, and comfortably furnished. Financial institutions have excellent alarm systems and many built-in features that offer protection to workers and facilities. Although the work is not physically strenuous, tellers do have to spend much of their time on their feet. The work clerks and others perform is usually of a very repetitive nature, and the duties are very similar from day to day. Most of the work is paperwork, computer entry, data processing, and other mechanical processes. Clerks do not frequently have contact with customers or clients. Tellers, on the other hand, have extended contact with the public and must always remain polite, even under trying circumstances. Tellers, clerks, and others must be able to work closely with each other, sometimes on joint tasks, as well as under supervision.

OUTLOOK

The DOL predicts that employment for financial institution tellers will grow more slowly than the average for all careers through 2018.

Despite this prediction, opportunities should be favorable for tellers. Until recently, there was a projected decline caused by competition from companies offering bank-like services, the increasing use of automatic teller machines, banking by telephone and computer, and other factors. However, the increasing number of bank branches, together with longer hours and more services offered to draw in more customers, will require more tellers. Prospects will be best for tellers who have excellent customer skills and are knowledgeable about a variety of financial services. Many job openings for tellers will come from the need to replace those who have left the field.

Employment for bookkeeping, accounting, and auditing clerks is expected to grow about as fast as the average for all occupations through 2018. Mergers and the use of computers and automated technologies will contribute to containing the number of new positions available. Due to their repetitive natures, turnover in these jobs is high. Many job openings will come from the need to find replacement workers for those who have left the field.

FOR MORE INFORMATION

The ABA has general information about the banking industry and information on education available through the American Institute of Banking.

American Bankers Association (ABA)
1120 Connecticut Avenue, NW
Washington, DC 20036-3902
Tel: 800-226-5377
http://www.aba.com

BAI offers a number of online courses such as "Introduction to Checks" and "Cash Handling Techniques." For more information, visit its Web site.

BAI
115 South LaSalle Street, Suite 3300
Chicago, IL 60603-3801
Tel: 800-224-9889
E-mail: info@bai.org
http://www.bai.org

Financial Planners

OVERVIEW

Financial planning is the process of establishing financial goals and creating ways to reach them. Certified *financial planners* examine the assets of their clients and suggest what steps they need to take in the future to meet their goals. They take a broad approach to financial advice, which distinguishes them from other professional advisers, such as insurance agents, stockbrokers, accountants, attorneys, and real estate agents, each of whom typically focuses on only one aspect of a person's finances. Approximately 208,400 personal financial advisers are employed in the United States.

HISTORY

Except for the depression years of the 1930s and intermittent recessions, the United States economy expanded impressively after World War I. As the average American's income increased, so did lifestyle expectations. By the 21st century, vacations to Disney World, cell phones for everyone in the family, two or three cars in the garage, and thoughts of a financially worry-free retirement were not uncommon. But how do Americans meet such high expectations? More and more have begun turning to professionals—financial planners—who recommend financial strategies. According to a consumer survey done by the Certified Financial Planner Board of Standards (CFP Board), 42 percent of respondents said they had experience with financial planners. In addition, 25 percent were currently using the services of a financial planner. Fee-only planners were the most popular, with 47 percent

100

of respondents noting that they preferred to work with a financial planner who is compensated this way instead of by commission or other means. Fee-only financial planners represent a growing segment of the financial advising industry, but the profession as a whole is booming due to the deregulation of certain institutions dealing with money. Because of this deregulation, banks, brokerage firms, and insurance companies have been allowed to offer more financial services—including investment advice—to customers since 1999. This has created many job openings for planners who want to work for these businesses.

Other reasons for growth in this industry include the large number of people (baby boomers, born between 1945 and 1965) who are closing in on or reaching retirement age and taking stock of their assets. As boomers consider if they have enough money to pay for the retirement they want, more and more of them are turning to financial planners for advice about such things as annuities, long-term health insurance, and individual retirement accounts. Another factor that has spurred growth is the increased awareness people have about investing and other options because of the large amount of financial information now directed at the general public. Today commercials for brokerage firms, television talk shows with weekly money advice, and financial publications and Web sites all offer various news and tips about what the average person should do with his or her money. All this information can be overwhelming, and people turn to experts for help. According to the CFP Board's survey,

Learn More About It: Money Management

Brancato, Robin F. *Money: Getting It, Using It, and Avoiding the Traps.* Lanham, Md.: The Scarecrow Press Inc., 2007.

Butler, Tamsen. *The Complete Guide to Personal Finance: For Teenagers.* Ocala, Fla.: Atlantic Publishing Group Inc., 2010.

Holmberg, Joshua. *The Teen's Guide to Personal Finance: Basic Concepts in Personal Finance That Every Teen Should Know.* Bloomington, Ind.: iUniverse, 2008.

Kwas, Susan Estelle, and Kathleen Brown. *It's a Money Thing!: A Girl's Guide to Managing Money.* San Francisco: Chronicle Books, 2008.

Orman, Suze. *The Money Book for the Young, Fabulous & Broke.* New York: Riverhead Hardcover, 2007.

70 percent of respondents felt that financial advisers were a good source of information about financial products. As tax laws change, the world economy becomes more complex, and new technologies alter workforces, financial planners will continue to be in demand for their expert advice.

THE JOB

Financial planners advise their clients on many aspects of finance. Although they seem to be jacks-of-all-trades, certified financial planners do not work alone; they meet with their clients' other advisers, such as attorneys, accountants, trust officers, and investment bankers. Financial planners fully research their clients' overall financial picture. After meeting with the clients and their other advisers, certified financial planners analyze the data they have received and generate a written report that includes their recommendations on how the clients can best achieve their goals. This report details the clients' financial objectives, current income, investments, risk tolerance, expenses, tax returns, insurance coverage, retirement programs, estate plans, and other important information.

Financial planning is an ongoing process. The plan must be monitored and reviewed periodically so that adjustments can be made, if necessary, to assure that it continues to meet individual needs.

The plan itself is a set of recommendations and strategies for clients to use or ignore, and financial planners should be ready to answer hard questions about the integrity of the plans they map out. After all, they are dealing with all of the money and investments that people have worked a lifetime accruing.

People need financial planners for different things. Some might want life insurance, college savings plans, or estate planning. Sometimes these needs are triggered by changes in people's lives, such as retirement, death of a spouse, disability, marriage, birth of children, or job changes. Certified financial planners spend the majority of their time on the following topics: investment planning, retirement planning, tax planning, estate planning, and risk management. All of these areas require different types of financial knowledge, and planners are generally expected to be extremely competent in the disciplines of asset management, employee benefits, estate planning, insurance, investments, and retirement, according to the Certified Financial Planner Board of Standards. A financial planner must also have good interpersonal skills, since establishing solid client-planner relationships is essential to the planner's success. It also helps to have good communication skills, since even the best financial plan, if presented poorly to a client, can be rejected.

A financial planner explains the features of a savings plan to a couple.
(Jupiterimages/Getty Images)

Clients drive the job of financial planners. The advice planners provide depends on their clients' particular needs, resources, and priorities. Many people think they cannot afford or do not need a comprehensive financial plan. Certified financial planners must have a certain amount of expertise in sales to build their client base.

Certified financial planners use various ways to develop their client lists, including telephone solicitation, giving seminars on financial planning to the general public or specific organizations, and networking with social contacts. Referrals from satisfied customers also help the business grow.

Although certified financial planners are trained in comprehensive financial planning, some specialize in one area, such as asset management, investments, or retirement planning. In most small or self-owned financial planning companies, they are generalists. However, in some large companies, planners might specialize in particular areas, including insurance, real estate, mutual funds, annuities, pensions, or business valuations.

REQUIREMENTS
High School
If financial planning sounds interesting to you, take as many business classes as possible as well as mathematics. Communication courses,

such as speech or drama, will help put you at ease when talking in front of a crowd, something financial planners must do occasionally. English courses will help you prepare the written reports planners present to their clients.

Postsecondary Training

Earning a bachelor's degree starts financial planners on the right track, but it will help if your degree indicates a skill with numbers, be it in science or business. A business administration degree with a specialization in financial planning or a liberal arts degree with courses in accounting, business administration, economics, finance, marketing, human behavior, counseling, and public speaking is excellent preparation for this sort of job.

Certification or Licensing

Education alone will not motivate clients to easily turn over their finances to you. Many financial professionals are licensed on the state and federal levels in financial planning specialties, such as stocks and insurance. The U.S. Securities and Exchange Commission and most states have licensing requirements for investment advisers, a category under which most financial planners also fall. However, most of the activities of planners are not regulated by the government. Therefore, to show credibility to clients, most financial planners choose to become certified as either a certified financial planner (CFP) or a chartered financial consultant (ChFC).

To receive the CFP mark of certification, offered by the CFP Board, candidates must meet what the board refers to as the four E's, which comprise the following.

Education. To be eligible to take the certification exam, candidates must meet education requirements in one of the following ways. The first option is to complete a CFP board-registered program in financial planning. The second is to hold a specific degree and professional credentials in one of several areas the board has approved of; these include certified public accountant, licensed attorney, chartered financial consultant, chartered life underwriter, chartered financial analyst, doctor of business administration, and Ph.D. in business or economics. Lastly, applicants may submit transcripts of their undergraduate or graduate education to the board for review. If the board feels the education requirements have been met, the candidate may sit for the exam. Additionally, applicants must have a bachelor's degree in any area of study or program to obtain CFP certification. They do not need to have earned this degree at the time they take the examination, but must show proof of completion of this degree in order to complete the final stage of certification.

Examination. Once candidates have completed the education requirements, they may take the certification exam, which tests knowledge on various key aspects of financial planning.

Experience. Either before or after passing the certification exam, candidates must have three years of work experience.

Ethics. After candidates have completed the education, examination, and experience requirements, they must voluntarily ascribe to the CFP Board's Code of Ethics and Professional Responsibility and Financial Planning Practice Standards to be allowed to use the CFP mark. This voluntary agreement empowers the board to take action if a CFP licensee violates the code. Such violations could lead to disciplinary action, including permanent revocation of the right to use the CFP mark.

The American College offers the ChFC designation. To receive this designation, candidates must complete certain course work stipulated by The American College, meet experience requirements, and agree to uphold The American College's Code of Ethics and Procedures. To maintain the CFP and the ChFC designations, professionals will need to meet continuing education and other requirements as determined by the CFP Board and The American College.

Three other organizations offer certification to financial planning professionals. Fi360 offers the accredited investment fiduciary and accredited investment fiduciary analyst designations. The Investment Management Consultants Association offers the following designations: certified investment management analyst and chartered private wealth adviser. The Accreditation Council for Accountancy and Taxation confers the accredited retirement adviser designation. Contact these organizations for more information.

Other Requirements

Other factors that contribute to success as a financial planner include keeping up with continuing education, referrals from clients, specialization, people and communication skills, and a strong educational background.

EXPLORING

There is not much that students can do to explore this field, since success as a certified financial planner comes only with training and years on the job. However, you can check out the financial planning information available on the Internet to familiarize yourself with the terms used in the industry. You should also take as many finance and business classes as possible. Talking to certified financial planners will also help you gather information on the field.

EMPLOYERS

Approximately 208,400 personal financial advisers are employed in the United States. They work for financial planning firms across the country. Many of these firms are small, perhaps employing two to 15 people, and most are located in urban areas. A smaller, but growing, number of financial planners are employed by corporations, banks, credit unions, mutual fund companies, insurance companies, accounting or law firms, colleges and universities, credit counseling organizations, and brokerage firms. In addition, many financial planners are self-employed.

STARTING OUT

Early in their careers, financial planners work for banks, mutual fund companies, or investment firms and usually receive extensive on-the-job training. The job will deal heavily with client-based and research activities. Financial planners may start their own business as they learn personal skills and build their client base. During their first few years, certified financial planners spend many hours analyzing documents, meeting with other advisers, and networking to find new clients.

ADVANCEMENT

Those who have not changed their career track in five years can expect to have established some solid, long-term relationships with clients. Measured success at this point will be the planners' service fees, which will be marked up considerably from when they started their careers.

Those who have worked in the industry for 10 years usually have many clients and a six-figure income. Experienced financial planners can also move into careers in investment banking, financial consulting, and financial analysis. Because people skills are also an integral part of being a financial planner, consulting, on both personal and corporate levels, is also an option. Many planners will find themselves attending business school, either to achieve a higher income or to switch to one of the aforementioned professions.

EARNINGS

There are several methods of compensation for financial planners. Fee-only means that compensation is earned entirely from fees from consultation, plan development, or investment management. These fees may be charged on an hourly or project basis depending on clients' needs or on a percentage of assets under management. Commission-only compensation is received from the sale of financial products that clients agree to purchase to implement financial planning recommendations. There is no charge for advice or preparation of the financial plan. Fee-offset means that compensation received in the form of commission from the sale of financial products is offset against fees charged for the planning process. Combination fee/commission is a fee charged for consultation, advice, and financial plan preparation on an hourly, project, or percentage basis. Planners might also receive commissions from recommended products targeted to achieve goals and objectives. Some planners work on a salary basis for financial services institutions such as banks, credit unions, and other related organizations.

The median annual gross income of certified financial planners was $215,345 in 2009, according to the *2009 Survey of Trends in the Financial Planning Industry,* which was conducted by the College for Financial Planning. These incomes were earned from financial plan writing, product sales, consulting, and related activities.

The U.S. Department of Labor (DOL) reports that financial planners earned a median annual salary of $68,200 in 2009. The most experienced financial planners with the highest level of education earned more than $166,400, while the least experienced financial planners earned less than $33,790.

Firms might also provide beginning financial planners with a steady income by paying a draw, which is a minimum salary based on the commission and fees the planner can be expected to earn.

Some financial planners receive vacation days, sick days, and health insurance, but that depends on whether they work for financial institutions or on their own.

WORK ENVIRONMENT

Most financial planners work by themselves in offices or at home. Others work in offices with other financial planners. Established financial planners usually work the same hours as others in the business community. Beginners who are seeking customers probably work longer hours. Many planners accommodate customers by meeting with them in the evenings and on weekends. They might spend a lot of time out of the office meeting with current and prospective clients, attending civic functions, and participating in trade association meetings.

OUTLOOK

Employment for financial planners is expected to grow much faster than the average for all careers through 2018, according to the DOL. Strong employment growth is expected for a number of reasons. More funds should be available for investment, as the economy, personal income, and inherited wealth grow. Demographics will also play a role; as increasing numbers of baby boomers turn 50, demand will grow for retirement-related investments. Most people, in general, are likely to turn to financial planners for assistance with retirement planning. Individual saving and investing for retirement are expected to become more important, as many companies reduce pension benefits and switch from defined-benefit retirement plans to defined-contribution plans, which shift the investment responsibility from the company to the individual. Furthermore, a growing number of individual investors are expected to seek advice from financial planners regarding the increasing complexity and array of investment alternatives for assistance with estate planning.

Due to the highly competitive nature of financial planning, many beginners leave the field because they are not able to establish a sufficient clientele. Once established, however, planners have a strong attachment to their occupation because of high earning potential and considerable investment in training. Job opportunities should be best for mature individuals with successful work experience.

FOR MORE INFORMATION

For more information about financial education and the ChFC designation, contact
The American College
270 South Bryn Mawr Avenue
Bryn Mawr, PA 19010-2105
Tel: 610-526-1000
http://www.theamericancollege.edu

To learn more about financial planning and to obtain a copy of the Guide to CFP Certification, contact
Certified Financial Planner Board of Standards
1425 K Street, NW, Suite 500

Washington, DC 20005-3686
Tel: 800-487-1497
http://www.cfp.net

For information on financial planning, visit the association's Web site.
Financial Planning Association
4100 East Mississippi Avenue, Suite 400
Denver, CO 80246-3053
Tel: 800-322-4237
http://www.fpanet.org

For information about certification, contact
Investment Management Consultants Association
5619 DTC Parkway, Suite 500
Greenwood Village, CO 80111-3044
Tel: 303-770-3377
E-mail: imca@imca.org
http://www.imca.org

For more information on fee-only financial advisers, contact
National Association of Personal Financial Advisors
3250 North Arlington Heights Road, Suite 109
Arlington Heights, IL 60004-1574
Tel: 847-483-5400
E-mail: info@napfa.org
http://www.napfa.org

INTERVIEW

Neil Brown is a fee-only certified financial planner (CFP) with Burkett Financial Services, LLC in West Columbia, South Carolina. He has been a CFP practitioner since 1997. In addition, Neil is a certified public accountant (CPA) and the program coordinator for and an instructor in the CFP certification education program at Midlands Technical College. He also assists in Youth Corps, a program that educates teens about life topics, including financial issues. Neil was kind enough to discuss his career with the editors of Careers in Focus: Financial Services.

Q. Why did you decide to become a financial planner?

A. My greatest reason for becoming a financial planner was to help people. We have too many people who have the ability to make money but not to accumulate it, invest it, and spend it wisely in retirement. My main reason for getting into this field was my interest in my own financial progress and then more so in others. While my clients are high net-worth or high income and do not spend more than they make, many people don't have that luxury and I try to help them as well even if I don't take them on as a client and charge them for it. If someone is willing to ask, I am willing to answer whether they are a client or not. I saw my family growing up do so much with so little and wondered how people with so much could do so little and then realized it is simply on what they know about using money wisely.

Q. What do you like most and least about your job?

A. My favorite part of my job is my interaction with my clients and helping them lay out a path to reach their goals in life. My least favorite part of my job is what I can't control. For example, the 2008 markets put a damper on everyone, even those who pay for financial advice, and I just have to realize that goals have to change given the downturns we have in life.

Q. What advice would you give to high school students who are interested in this career?

A. I think the best thing is to get a subscription to a basic magazine like *Kiplinger's* and begin to implement small things in their own lives (i.e., start a small savings account for a rainy day, begin to plan for college, establish credit when you can and use it wisely). I would also suggest talking with your parents or teachers and if they don't have answers, finding them together. Many parents raise money-knowledge-deficient children because they don't know themselves. Students can ask their economic teachers to bring in a guest speaker. I speak at several schools in my area just on very basic stuff and it is amazing what students don't know or their parents don't know.

Q. What are the three most important professional qualities for financial planners?

A. First, the ability to listen and understand a client is extremely important. It does not matter how technically competent you are if you cannot actually communicate with clients.

Second, excellent technical skills are required. We have to be masters of many disciplines—estate tax, income tax, investments, insurance (life, disability, long-term care, health, property, etc.), retirement law and modeling, education planning, and so many more. I spend at least 30 to 40 hours per month reading and studying to keep up in my field.

Third would be adaptation. Our discipline is not a science. It is both art and science. We have to be able to apply what we know to situations where there is no correct answer. This is not compliance of taxes but applying many areas into a comprehensive solution without adversely affecting other areas of the plan.

Q. What are your duties and responsibilities as the program coordinator and an instructor in the Midlands Tech CFP program?

A. I coordinate and am the lead instructor for two CFP educational programs for mostly business professionals. They take an 18-month program in financial calculator usage, insurance, retirement, investments, income tax, and estate tax, and then finish with a case study class. At the end, they are qualified to sit for the CFP Examination and hopefully pass and practice as such.

Q. Is certification required for financial planners? How important is certification to career success in the field?

A. Unfortunately anyone can hang out a shingle and call themselves a financial planner. Certification is not a requirement, but I would never suggest going to a non-CFP for financial planning just as I would never suggest going to a non-CPA or non-attorney for tax or legal advice. On the flip side, certification does not guarantee a qualified planner either, but it at least shows an individual's initiative to achieve the basic skills required.

Q. Tell us more about your work in the Youth Corps.

A. I am involved in Youth Corps for ninth and 10th graders. It is a yearlong program for specific students nominated and selected for participation. They meet with numerous professionals regarding all kinds of activities from arts and media to finances and volunteerism. My area is finance and introduction of such to them. Our section (40 hours in length) will be held next March. We have five members on our finance team and will discuss budgeting, savings, checking, investing, and other topics to introduce young people to areas in which they may not be familiar.

Q. What is the future of financial planning?

A. I think the future is bright. The coming decades will see the largest transfer of wealth from generation to generation in history. These people will need help in all areas noted above. I do see a shake out where those who don't spend the hours in study and don't take the client's best interest at heart will fail. I see firms trying and failing to get into financial planning because there will be those who champion client interests and others who will not gain the respect that is needed to be a true professional.

Financial Services Brokers

OVERVIEW

Financial services brokers, sometimes called *registered representatives, account executives, securities sales representatives,* or *stockbrokers,* work to represent both individuals and organizations who wish to invest in and sell stocks, bonds, or other financial products. Financial services brokers analyze companies offering stocks to see if investing is worth the risk. They also advise clients on proper investment strategies for their own investment goals. Securities, commodities, and financial services brokers hold approximately 317,200 jobs in the United States.

HISTORY

When a government wants to build a new sewer system or a company wants to build a new factory, it rarely has the required money—or capital—readily at hand to do it. It must first raise the capital from investors. Historically, raising capital to finance the needs of government and commerce was—and often still is—an arduous task. European monarchies, particularly during the 18th and 19th centuries, relied heavily upon bankers to meet the costs of the interminable wars that devastated the continent and to assist in early industrial expansion. This system grew obsolete, however, and governments, banks, and industry turned to the burgeoning middle class for funds. They offered middle class investors securities and stocks—a fractional ownership in a company or enterprise—in exchange for their money. Soon, dealers emerged that linked

QUICK FACTS

School Subjects
Business
Mathematics

Personal Skills
Communication/ideas
Technical/scientific

Work Environment
Primarily indoors
Primarily one location

Minimum Education Level
Bachelor's degree

Salary Range
$29,980 to $66,930 to
$166,400+

Certification or Licensing
Required by certain states

Outlook
About as fast as the average

DOT
250

GOE
13.01.01

NOC
1113

O*NET-SOC
41–3031.00, 41–3031.01

government and industry with the smaller investor. In the United States, the New York Stock Exchange was formed in 1790 and officially established in 1817.

The stock exchange functions as a marketplace where stockbrokers buy and sell securities for individuals or institutions. Stock prices can fluctuate from minute to minute, with the price of a stock at any given time determined by the demand for it. As a direct result of the disastrous stock market crash of 1929, the federal Securities

Fun Facts About Federal Reserve Notes

- The Bureau of Engraving and Printing prints all of the Federal Reserve Notes (or paper money) used in the United States. Today, it has approximately 1,900 employees in Washington, D.C., and Fort Worth, Texas.

- The bureau produced 26 million notes a day in 2010, which had a face value of approximately $974 million.

- Currency paper is made up of 75 percent cotton and 25 percent linen.

- $1 notes made up approximately 42 percent of all currency printed by the bureau in 2009.

- All paper money wears out eventually from everyday use. The bureau estimates the following life spans by note: $1 (42 months), $5 (16 months), $10 (18 months), $20 (24 months), $50 (55 months), and $100 (89 months).

- Who's who on our nation's paper currency? George Washington = $1, Thomas Jefferson = $2, Abraham Lincoln = $5, Alexander Hamilton = $10, Andrew Jackson = $20, Ulysses Grant = $50, and Benjamin Franklin = $100. Dignitaries on higher denominations (which are no longer produced) include William McKinley = $500, Grover Cleveland = $1,000, James Madison = $5,000, Salmon Chase = $10,000, and Woodrow Wilson = $100,000.

- It's a man's world. Martha Washington—the wife of our nation's first president—is the only woman whose portrait has appeared on U.S. paper currency. Her portrait appeared on the face of the $1 Silver Certificate of 1886 and 1891, and the back of the $1 Silver Certificate of 1896.

Source: U.S. Department of the Treasury, Bureau of Engraving and Printing (http://moneyfactory.gov)

Exchange Act of 1934 set up a federal commission to control the handling of securities and made illegal any manipulation of prices on stock exchanges. Today, the public is protected by regulations that set standards for stock listings, require public disclosure of the financial condition of companies offering stock, and prohibit stock manipulation and trading on inside information.

THE JOB

The most important part of a broker's job is finding customers and building a client base. Beginning brokers spend much of their time searching for customers, relying heavily on telephone solicitation such as "cold calls"—calling people with whom they have never had any contact. Brokers also find customers through business and social contacts or they might be given a list of likely prospects from their brokerage firm.

When financial services brokers open accounts for new customers, they first record all the personal information that is required to allow the customer to trade securities through the brokerage firm. Depending on a customer's knowledge of the market, the broker may explain the meaning of stock market terms and trading practices and offer financial counseling. Then the broker helps the customer to devise an individual financial portfolio, including securities, life insurance, corporate and municipal bonds, mutual funds, certificates of deposit, annuities, and other investments. The broker must determine the customer's investment goals—such as whether the customer wants long-term, steady growth or a quick turnaround of stocks for short-term gains—and then offers advice on investments accordingly. Once an investment strategy has been developed, brokers execute buy and sell orders for their customers by relaying the information electronically to the floor of the stock exchange, where the order is put into effect by the broker's floor representative. Securities traders also buy and sell securities, but usually as a representative of a private firm.

From the research department of the brokerage firm, brokers obtain information on the activities and projected growth of any company that is currently offering stock or plans to offer stock in the near future. The actual or perceived strength of a company is a major factor in a stock-purchase decision. Brokers must be prepared to answer questions on the technical aspects of stock market operations and also be informed on current economic conditions. They are expected to have the market knowledge to anticipate certain trends and to counsel customers accordingly in terms of their particular stock holdings.

Some financial services brokers specialize in areas such as institutional accounts, bond issues, or mutual funds. Whatever their area of specialization, financial services brokers must keep abreast of all significant political and economic conditions that might effect financial markets, maintain very accurate records for all transactions, and continually solicit new customers.

REQUIREMENTS

High School
If you are interested in becoming a financial services broker, you should take courses in business, accounting, economics, mathematics, government, and communications.

Postsecondary Training
Because of the specialized knowledge necessary to perform this job properly, a college education is increasingly important, especially in the larger brokerage houses. To make intelligent and insightful judgments, a broker must be able to read and understand financial reports and evaluate statistics. For this reason, although employers seldom require specialized academic training, a bachelor's degree in business administration, economics, accounting, or finance is helpful.

Certification or Licensing
Almost all states require brokers to be licensed. Some states administer written examinations and some require brokers to post a personal bond. Brokers must register as representatives of their firms with the Financial Industry Regulatory Authority (FINRA). In order to register with FINRA, brokers must first pass the General Securities Registered Representative Examination (Series 7 exam) to demonstrate competence in the areas in which they will work. In addition, they must be employees of a registered firm for at least four months. Many states also require brokers to take and pass a second examination—the Uniform Securities Agents State Law Examination (Series 63 or 66).

Other Requirements
Because they deal with the public, brokers should be well groomed and pleasant and have large reserves of tact and patience. Employers look for ambitious individuals with sales ability. Brokers also need self-confidence and the ability to handle frequent rejections. Above all, they must have a highly developed sense of responsibility,

because in many instances they will be handling funds that represent a client's life savings.

EXPLORING

Any sales experience can provide you with a general background for work in financial services. You might be able to find summer employment in a brokerage house. A visit to a local investment office, the New York Stock Exchange, or one of the commodities exchanges located in other major cities will provide a valuable opportunity to observe how transactions are handled and what is required of people in the field.

EMPLOYERS

Financial services brokers and related workers hold approximately 317,200 jobs. The U.S. Department of Labor (DOL) reports that 49 percent work for securities and commodities firms, exchanges, and investment services companies. Other employers include banks, savings institutions, and credit unions. Approximately 15 percent of financial services brokers are self-employed.

Financial services brokers work all around the country. Although many employers are very small, the largest employers of financial services brokers are a few large firms that have their main offices in major cities, especially New York.

STARTING OUT

Many firms hire beginning sales workers and train and retain them for a probationary period to determine their talents and ability to succeed in the business. The training period lasts about six months and includes classroom instruction and on-the-job training. Applications for these beginning jobs may be made directly to the personnel offices of the various securities firms. Check your local Yellow Pages or the Internet for listings of securities firms.

ADVANCEMENT

Depending upon their skills and ambitions, financial services brokers may advance rapidly in this field. Accomplished brokers may find that the size and number of accounts they service will increase to a point at which they no longer need to solicit new customers.

Others become branch managers, research analysts, or partners in their own firms.

EARNINGS

The salaries of trainees and beginners range from $1,200 to $1,500 per month, although larger firms pay a somewhat higher starting wage. Once the financial services broker has acquired a sufficient number of accounts, he or she works solely on a commission basis, with fees resulting from the size and type of security bought or sold. Some firms pay annual bonuses to their brokers when business warrants. Since earnings can fluctuate greatly based on the condition of the market, some brokers may find it necessary to supplement their income through other means during times of slow market activity.

According to the DOL, the median earnings for brokers were $66,930 a year in 2009. Ten percent earned less than $29,980, and 10 percent earned more than $166,400.

Benefits for full-time workers include vacation and sick time, health, and sometimes dental, insurance, and pension or 401(k) plans. Self-employed financial services brokers must provide their own benefits.

WORK ENVIRONMENT

Brokers work more flexible hours than workers in other fields. They may work fewer hours during slow trading periods but be required to put in overtime dealing with paperwork during busy periods.

The atmosphere of a brokerage firm is frequently highly charged, and the peaks and drops of market activity can produce a great deal of tension. Watching fortunes being made is exciting, but the reverse occurs frequently, too, and it requires responsibility and maturity to weather the setbacks.

OUTLOOK

The DOL predicts that job opportunities for financial services brokers are expected to grow about as fast as the average for all occupations through 2018 because of continued interest in the stock market and the increasing number and variety of financial products. Rising personal incomes and greater inherited wealth are increasing the amount of funds people are able to invest. Many people dabble in investing via their personal computers and the Internet. Even those with limited means have the option of investing through a variety of methods such as investment clubs, mutual funds, and monthly payment plans. In addition, the expansion of business activities and new technological breakthroughs will create increased demand for the sale of stock to meet capital requirements for companies around the world.

Employment growth in this field will be offset somewhat as a result of major industry consolidation caused by the recent financial crisis.

Demand for financial services brokers fluctuates with the economy. Turnover among beginners is high because they have a hard time soliciting enough clients. Because of potentially high earnings, competition in this business is very intense. Opportunities will be strongest for those with undergraduate degrees from top universities, certification, and excellent grades in accounting, business, economics, and finance classes. Brokers with master's degree in business or finance will have the strongest job prospects.

FOR MORE INFORMATION

For information on industry regulation, contact
Financial Industry Regulatory Authority
1735 K Street, NW
Washington, DC 20006-1506
Tel: 301-590-6500
http://www.finra.org

To learn more about investing, the securities industry, and industry issues, contact
Securities Industry and Financial Markets Association
120 Broadway, 35th Floor
New York, NY 10271-0080
Tel: 212-313-1200
http://www.sifma.org

Forensic Accountants and Auditors

QUICK FACTS

School Subjects
Business
Mathematics

Personal Skills
Communication/ideas
Leadership/management

Work Environment
Primarily indoors
One location with some
travel

Minimum Education Level
Bachelor's degree

Salary Range
$37,690 to $60,340 to
$104,450+

Certification or Licensing
Recommended

Outlook
Much faster than the average

DOT
160

GOE
04.04.02

NOC
1111

O*NET-SOC
13-2011.00

OVERVIEW

Forensic accountants and auditors, sometimes known as *investigative accountants, investigative auditors,* and *certified fraud examiners,* use accounting principles and theories to support or oppose claims being made in litigation. Like other accountants and auditors, these professionals are trained to analyze and verify financial records. However, forensic accountants and auditors use these skills to identify and document financial wrongdoing. They prepare reports that may be used in criminal and civil trials. The word "forensic" means "suitable for a court of law, public debate, or formal argumentation." There are approximately 1.3 million accountants and auditors, a category that includes forensic accountants and auditors, employed in the United States.

HISTORY

People have used accounting and bookkeeping procedures for as long as they have engaged in trade. Records of accounts have been preserved from ancient and medieval times.

Modern bookkeeping dates back to the advent of double-entry bookkeeping, a method of tracking the impact of transactions on both a company's assets and profitability. Double-entry bookkeeping was developed in medieval Italy. The earliest known published work about this system was written in 1494 by an Italian monk named Luca Pacioli. Pacioli did not invent the system, but he did summarize principles that remain largely unchanged today.

Records preserved from 16th century Europe indicate that formulations were developed during that time to account for assets, liabilities, and income. When the Industrial Revolution swept through the world in the 18th century, accounting became even more sophisticated to accommodate the acceleration of financial transactions caused by mechanization and mass production.

In the 20th and 21st centuries, accounting has become a more creative and interesting discipline. Computers now perform many routine computations, while accountants tend to spend more time interpreting the results. Many accountants now hold senior management positions within large organizations. They assess the possible impact of various transactions, mergers, and acquisitions and help companies manage their employees more efficiently.

While people have probably investigated financial records for as long as people have kept accounts, forensic accounting did not emerge as a distinct area of specialty until quite recently. The increased litigation and white-collar crime that emerged in the 1980s (and continues today) has contributed to rapid growth in this field.

A forensic accountant testifies during a trial. *(Jeremy Wadsworth, AP Photo)*

Areas of Focus for
Forensic Accountants and Auditors

- Asset misappropriation
- Bankruptcy fraud
- Check kiting
- Contract and procurement fraud
- Credit card fraud
- Embezzlement
- Employee fraud investigation
- Financial statement fraud
- Insurance claims
- Money laundering
- Securities fraud
- Telemarketing fraud
- Violations of Generally Accepted Accounting Principles
- Violations of Generally Accepted Auditing Standards

Source: National Association of Forensic Accountants

THE JOB

Forensic accountants and auditors have all the skills possessed by traditional accountants and auditors. They are trained to compile, verify, and analyze financial records and taxes. They monitor the efficiency of business procedures and management. Unlike traditional accounting and auditing professionals, however, forensic accountants and auditors use their skills to help clients prepare for trials. They follow paper trails of financial documents to prepare reports for clients to use in litigation.

"Forensic accounting," says Jim DiGabriele, of DiGabriele, McNulty, Campanella & Co., "uses investigative skills to follow paper trails. We follow financial documents to the end of the trail and then we more or less prepare reports for litigation."

In an investigation, the forensic accountant usually begins by reviewing relevant financial and business documents and interviewing the people involved. He or she also may assemble relevant third-party information, such as economic data for comparable industries or companies. Using the compiled information, the forensic accountant may then calculate the losses or damages caused by any financial violations or errors. Finally, the forensic accountant prepares a detailed report explaining his or her findings and conclusions. This report is intended for use in litigation.

Experts estimate that one in 20 cases go to litigation, but accountants must treat every case as if it is going to trial in order to provide comprehensive information to their employer.

If a case is scheduled to proceed to litigation, the attorneys involved may schedule a deposition. A deposition is a pretrial hearing, in which attorneys from both sides may interview one another's witnesses to gain information about the case. Forensic accountants sometimes help attorneys prepare questions for these depositions. They also are sometimes asked to answer questions in a deposition.

If and when a case finally goes to trial, a forensic accountant also may serve as an expert witness and testify before the court. Forensic accountants may offer testimony regarding the nature of the violation, a person's or company's guilt or innocence, and the amount of the resulting damages. As expert witnesses, forensic accountants must be able to present information in a clear and organized manner. They must be able to explain complicated accounting concepts in a way that can be understood by people who are not in the field. They must be able to explain and defend the methods they used to arrive at their conclusions.

There is no "typical" case for a forensic accountant. Forensic accountants use their skills to investigate a wide variety of situations or violations.

Many insurance companies hire forensic accountants to evaluate claims they suspect may be inflated or fraudulent. If an insured company files a claim for a business interruption loss, for example, the insurance company may hire a forensic accountant to make sure the company's loss was as great as the company claims it was. To make this assessment, the forensic accountant must review the company's past financial records. Before calculating the company's probable loss, the forensic accountant also must consider the current marketplace. If the economy is booming and the market for the company's products or services is hot, the insured's losses may be substantial. If the economy is sluggish, or if the company's product has become obsolete, the losses may be much lower.

Insurance companies also hire forensic accountants to assess claimants' loss of income due to accidents or disability, or property loss to fire, flood, or theft. Occasionally, a claimant may hire a forensic accountant to defend his or her claim or to rebut another forensic accountant's testimony.

Forensic accountants also investigate malpractice claims against accountants or auditors. In these cases, forensic accountants must examine the reports prepared by the accountants and auditors to determine whether they followed accepted procedures. If the forensic accountant does discover an error, he or she also may be required to calculate the financial impact of the discrepancy.

Companies sometimes hire forensic accountants to determine whether employees are taking bribes from vendors or customers in return for offering higher payments or lower prices. Companies also hire forensic accountants to detect insider trading. Insider trading occurs when an employee uses privileged information to make a profit—or helps someone else make a profit—by buying or selling stock. Forensic accountants also assist corporate clients by calculating loss due to breach of contract, patent infringement, and fraud.

Some forensic accountants engage in divorce valuation work. These professionals determine the value of the personal assets, liabilities, pensions, and business holdings of individuals involved in a divorce settlement.

REQUIREMENTS

High School

If you are interested in entering this field, take as many math and computer classes as possible in high school. You also should take any available business classes, because forensic accountants and auditors must understand basic business procedures in order to assess business interruption losses. Forensic accountants and auditors who eventually form their own firms also will need management and administrative skills. Business classes can offer you a solid foundation in these areas.

Writing, speech, and communication classes are extremely useful courses to take. A forensic accountant's value to clients depends entirely on his or her ability to provide credible reports and convincing testimony for trial. For this reason, forensic accountants must be able to write clear, organized reports. They must be able to speak clearly and audibly in courtrooms. They must appear poised and confident when speaking publicly, and they must be able to convey complicated information in comprehensible language.

Postsecondary Training

Once in college, you should major in accounting or major in business administration with a minor in accounting. It is important to remember that you will not graduate from college as a forensic accountant or auditor. You will first work as a general accountant or auditor and then learn the skills necessary to be a forensic accountant or auditor through experience. Also included in your course of study should be computer classes, as well as English or communication classes. In the past several years, a few colleges (such as Carlow University, Franklin University, Mount Marty College, Myers University, and Waynesburg College) have started offering degrees and concentrations in forensic accounting, but most students still prepare for this field by majoring in accounting and learning forensic accounting techniques on the job.

Some organizations prefer to hire accountants and auditors with master's degrees in accounting or master's in business administration. So, depending on what company you want to work for, you may need to continue your education beyond the college level.

Certification or Licensing

Anyone who is interested in becoming a forensic accountant should first become a certified public accountant (CPA). While it is theoretically possible to practice as a forensic accountant without becoming a CPA, it is extremely unlikely that anyone would succeed in so doing. Clients hire forensic accountants with the idea that they may eventually serve as expert witnesses. A forensic accountant who is not certified could be easily discredited in a trial.

To become a CPA, most states require candidates to have completed 150 credit hours, or the equivalent of a master's degree, in an accounting program of study. The American Institute of Certified Public Accountants (AICPA) is working to make this a national standard for accounting education as accounting procedures and reporting laws become increasingly more complex. Candidates for the credential also must pass the Uniform CPA Examination, which is developed by the AICPA. Finally, many states require candidates to have a certain amount of professional experience (usually at least two years) to qualify for certification. Most states also require CPAs to earn about 40 hours of continuing education each year.

AICPA members who have valid CPA certificates may also earn the following specialty designations: accredited in business valuation, certified in financial forensics, certified information technology professional, and personal financial specialist.

A CPA who has gained some experience should consider becoming a certified fraud examiner (CFE). Forensic accountants and fraud examiners use many of the same skills. In fact, the titles are sometimes used interchangeably, although, according to the National

Association of Forensic Accountants (NAFA), fraud examiners are more often concerned with developing procedures and implementing measures to prevent fraud. However, the two areas are not mutually exclusive; many forensic accountants also work as fraud examiners and vice versa. To gain the CFE designation, a CPA must meet certain educational and professional experience requirements and pass the Uniform CFE Examination, which is administered by the Association of Certified Fraud Examiners. The designation can help forensic accountants establish their credibility as expert witnesses. CFEs must complete a certain amount of continuing education each year.

The National Association of Forensic Accountants also offers certification to its members. Contact the association for more information.

Other Requirements

Forensic accountants and auditors are the sleuths of the financial world. Consequently, they must be curious and dogged in their pursuit of answers. They must have exceptional attention to detail and be capable of intense concentration. Like every professional involved with the judicial system, forensic accountants and auditors are frequently subject to abrupt schedule changes, so they also should be able to work under stressful conditions and meet exceptionally tight deadlines. They also need excellent communication skills, and they must be poised and confident.

EXPLORING

Opportunities for high school students to explore this field are limited. You may, however, contact people in this field to request information interviews. Information interviews can be an excellent way to learn about different careers. You can also visit Web sites that provide information on accounting. The American Institute of Certified Public Accountants offers an excellent Web site called Start Here Go Places in Business and Accounting (http://www.startheregoplaces .com) that provides information on careers, educational training, scholarships, internships, and the CPA Examination.

Hone your math skills outside of the classroom by joining your high school math team or by volunteering as a math tutor at your school or a local learning center. You can also improve your business and accounting skills by joining a school group that has a yearly budget and offering to be the treasurer. This will give you the opportunity to be responsible for an organization's financial records.

Try landing a summer job performing clerical tasks for accounting or law firms. This experience can help you become familiar with the documentation necessary in both fields. When in college, you should seek internship positions within accounting firms in order to gain practical experience and to make contacts within the industry.

EMPLOYERS

Approximately 1.3 million accountants and auditors (a category that includes forensic accountants and auditors) are employed in the United States. Forensic accountants and auditors usually work for accounting companies that provide litigation support for insurance companies, law firms, and other parties involved in litigation. Others are employed by government agencies and colleges and universities.

STARTING OUT

Most people spend several years working as accountants before specializing in forensic accounting. Their first hurdle after college is to find employment as an accountant. College professors and career services counselors can help accounting majors arrange interviews with respected accounting firms and government agencies. Students also can contact these firms and agencies directly to learn about job opportunities. Many accounting firms and government positions are advertised in newspapers and on the Internet.

In general, accounting firms tend to offer better starting salaries than government agencies. Larger firms also sometimes have entire departments dedicated to litigation support services. New graduates who secure positions with these firms might have opportunities to learn the forensic ropes while gaining experience as accountants. With time, after earning a CPA and gaining experience, an accountant within a large firm may have an opportunity to specialize in litigation support and forensic accounting. The largest firms include Pricewaterhouse Coopers, Ernst & Young, Deloitte Touche Tohmatsu, and KPMG International.

Another excellent way to gain relevant experience is by working for the Internal Revenue Service (IRS). IRS auditors and accountants use many of the same skills necessary for forensic accountants.

ADVANCEMENT

Forensic accountants and auditors usually advance by gaining experience and establishing reputations for integrity, thorough documentation, and reliable calculations. As a forensic accountant or auditor gains experience, he or she usually attracts more clients and is able to work on more interesting, complex cases. Experienced forensic accountants and auditors also can charge more per hour for their services, though, unless the individual is self-employed, this increase does not usually benefit the professional directly. With experience, forensic accountants and auditors also may gain opportunities to manage a litigation support department or to become a partners in an accounting firm. A significant number of forensic accountants and auditors also advance by leaving larger firms to establish their own companies.

EARNINGS

While there are no annual salary statistics specifically for forensic accountants and auditors, most of these professionals work within accounting firms and earn salaries that are commensurate with those of other accountants and auditors. According to the U.S. Department of Labor (DOL), the median annual earnings for accountants and auditors as a whole were $60,340 in 2009. The top paid 10 percent of accountants and auditors earned more than $104,450, and the bottom paid 10 percent earned less than $37,690. Partners in accounting firms can make even more. Naturally, salaries are affected by such factors as size of the firm, the level of the individual's education, and any certification he or she may have.

According to a survey conducted by the National Association of Colleges and Employers, entry-level public sector accountants who had bachelor's degrees received average starting salaries of $48,993 in 2009. Those in the private sector earned $46,684. Auditors in the public sector earned average starting salaries of $49,680, while those who worked in the private sector earned $48,228.

As forensic accountants become more experienced, they may earn slightly more than traditional accountants because many firms tend to charge premium rates for litigation support services. A forensic accountant's salary and bonus figures usually reflect, at least to some degree, the revenue they are generating for the accounting firm. For this reason, a forensic accountant's salary tends to grow as he or she gains experience. According to the National Association of Forensic Accountants, forensic accountants who had fewer than 10 years of experience charged between $80 and $140 per hour for their services. About 25 percent of those who had 11 to 15 years of experience charged between $141 and $170 per hour, and another 25 percent charged more than $170. Practitioners with between

16 and 20 years of experience charged between $171 and $200. In addition, 30 percent of those with more than 20 years of experience charged more than $200.

Most forensic accountants and auditors are employees who receive standard benefits such as paid vacation and sick days, health insurance, and 401(k) savings plans. Many who work for major accounting firms can also expect to earn bonuses based on their performance and the overall performance of their firm. Forensic accountants and auditors who become partners also may earn shares in the firm. Forensic accountants and auditors who act as self-employed consultants typically will not receive benefits and will have to provide their own health insurance and retirement plan.

WORK ENVIRONMENT

Forensic accountants and auditors typically work in bright, clean offices. A great deal of their work is done on computers and telephones, though most also occasionally travel to the offices of clients or those under investigation.

Because forensic accountants and auditors are hired to help clients prepare for trial, they often must work under tremendous pressure. They frequently encounter tight deadlines and changing schedules. Though forensic accountants and auditors generally work normal 40-hour weeks, they often work much longer hours as they prepare for a trial.

Forensic accountants and auditors also must contend with the pressures of serving as expert witnesses. Whenever they take the stand, they know that the attorneys for the other side of a case will attempt to discredit them and question their procedures and conclusions. Forensic accountants and auditors must be prepared to undergo extremely aggressive questioning. They must be able to remain calm and confident under trying circumstances.

OUTLOOK

The DOL predicts that employment for accountants and auditors will grow much faster than the average for all occupations through 2018. As the economy rebounds, more accountants will be needed to prepare books and taxes for new and growing companies. New accountants also will be needed to replace those who retire or change professions. Since about 1.3 million people currently work as accountants, the number of positions created by normal turnover should be significant.

The AICPA and the DOL call forensic accounting one of the hot growth areas for CPAs. One reason for this may be that the job is becoming well known due to high profile cases of financial mismanagement by formerly respected accounting firms such as Arthur Anderson. In this case, forensic accountants were among the experts that investigated the financial collapse of the previously stable company Enron and determined that obstruction of justice was committed by Arthur Andersen employees.

In our increasingly complex economy of business mergers, acquisitions, and failures, forensic accountants and auditors are increasingly in demand as companies rely on their services to determine if bankruptcy should be declared or if there is a way to remain solvent. The NAFA notes that the need for investigative accountants continues to increase in proportion to the insurance industry's growth and complexity. This is because insurance companies use these accountants' skills when determining how to settle claims, such as for business interruptions, inventory damage or loss, or any type of insurance claim where fraud may occur. Due to this demand, the overall outlook for forensic accountants and auditors should be good.

FOR MORE INFORMATION

For information on forensic careers and education, contact
American Academy of Forensic Sciences
410 North 21st Street
Colorado Springs, CO 80904-2712
Tel: 719-636-1100
http://www.aafs.org

Because forensic accountants are almost always certified public accountants, the institute is an excellent source of additional information.
American Institute of Certified Public Accountants
1211 Avenue of the Americas
New York, NY 10036-8775
Tel: 212-596-6200
http://www.aicpa.org

For information on careers, The Fraud Museum, scholarships, self-study courses, and the CFE designation, contact
Association of Certified Fraud Examiners
The Gregor Building
716 West Avenue

Austin, TX 78701-2727
Tel: 800-245-3321
E-mail: accounting@ACFE.com
http://www.acfe.com

For information on investigative accounting, contact
National Association of Forensic Accountants
6451 North Federal Highway, Suite 121
Fort Lauderdale, FL 33308-1487
Tel: 800-523-3680
E-mail: mail@nafanet.com
http://www.nafanet.com

For information on scholarships for college students and continuing education, contact
National Society of Accountants
Tel: 800-966-6679
http://www.nsacct.org

INTERVIEW

Frank Wisehart, MBA, CPA, ABV, CFE, CVA, is the director of business advisory services at Schneider Downs & Co. Inc. (http:// www.schneiderdowns.com). He has worked in the field of forensic accounting for the past 13 years. Frank discussed his career with the editors of Careers in Focus: Financial Services.

Q. Can you tell us a little about Schneider Downs & Co. Inc.?

A. Schneider Downs is an accounting, tax, and business advisory firm headquartered in Pittsburgh, Pennsylvania. Schneider Downs has one other office in Columbus, Ohio. I am the director of business advisory services at the Columbus location. We have about 340 total employees in the firm.

Q. Why did you decide to become a forensic accountant?

A. My grandfather was an attorney and my father is a practicing attorney. So, I have always been interested in the legal side of accounting.

An opportunity arose when I lost my job at Ernst & Young, LLP. I received a phone call asking if I would like to work on a temporary assignment in Port Huron, Michigan, on behalf of Merrill Lynch. Merrill Lynch was a major creditor at a regional manufacturing operation. The assignment was to last about two to four months. I was asked to review the books and records to search for improprieties by the prior business managers. We found some checks paid to the prior owners that were in transit, intercepted them, and recovered the money for Merrill. Ultimately, the temporary assignment turned into a five-year engagement. However, due to the temporary nature of the engagement, I decided that if I was going to be on my own for a while, I should become a certified fraud examiner (CFE). After adding the CFE designation by taking classes offered through the Association of Certified Fraud Examiners, I looked for other clients in need of a forensic accountant. I turned to attorneys I knew, worked on a few cases, and evolved into a forensic accounting and business valuation expert.

Q. Take us through a day in your life as a forensic accountant. What are your typical tasks/responsibilities?

A. On a typical day, I might receive literally a foot to a foot-and-one-half of detailed documentation. This would include items like bank statements, general ledgers, tax returns, billing statements, loan documents, e-mails, partnership agreements, and CDs containing other financial information. For example, after spending the better part of two days looking for evidence of say a fraudulent property transfer, I focused on a CD [that] contained encrypted QuickBooks data. We were able to find a program to circumvent the encryption, located the proper version of QuickBooks for the data set, loaded the file and, boom, all the data instantly appeared in the QuickBooks program. Using that data, we were able to tie the transaction descriptions to the tax returns. We were able to determine that the illegal transaction did not occur as the defendant had claimed; it occurred years after. As a result, the story told by the defendant about the circumstances of the transfer did not stand up.

Q. What do you like most and least about your job?

A. You search for hours through thousands of pages of information many times finding nothing to support your case. It can be boring and tedious, at times. However, when the case comes together it is very rewarding. It is very satisfying to present evidence about how someone committed a crime against another person(s) and watch them scramble to try to negotiate a deal.

It can be frustrating when your client expects you to find millions of dollars and you do not find anything close to what they think you should find. Sometimes, the evidence simply is not available or is so old, no one has kept the records we need.

Q. What are the three most important professional qualities for forensic accountants?

A. Good forensic accountants are part lawyer, part police officer, and part accountant. An understanding of how the legal aspects, criminal behavior, and flow of documentation work together is what separates the forensic professional from the general accountant. Forensic accountants start with a legal theory; for example, Joe removed money from the company. Next, we try to figure out how Joe might have removed the money, perhaps by paying fictitious companies that Joe secretly owned that did not perform any services for the company. Finally, we look for the documents to support the case such as false invoices submitted by the fictitious companies that Joe approved and the subsequent payment by the company for which Joe worked.

Q. What advice would you give to high school students who are interested in this career?

A. Most forensic accountants start as regular certified public accountants. I would suggest that high school students who are interested in this particular field of study help reconcile bank accounts for friends or family, become a member of the Association of Certified Fraud Examiners and, perhaps, help prepare or understand what small businesses do in order to prepare financial statements. A typical career starts in a certified public accounting firm as a staff auditor. This enables you to understand the underlying documents involved in running a business and preparing financial statements. In order to investigate financial crimes, you must have a good grasp of the underlying financial documentation.

Insurance Claims Representatives

OVERVIEW

Insurance claims representatives, or *claims adjusters,* investigate claims for personal, casualty, or property loss or damages. They determine the extent of the insurance company's liability and try to negotiate an out-of-court settlement with the claimant. There are approximately 294,600 claims adjusters employed in the United States.

HISTORY

Insurance is an action or process that insures a party against loss or damage by a contingent event, such as fire, accident, illness, or death. The field originated in the late 1600s at Lloyd's Coffeehouse in London as a means of sharing the risks of commercial voyages. Underwriters received a fee for the portion of the financial responsibility they shouldered.

Although organized insurance first developed with the maritime industry, the need for protection also grew in other areas. Life insurance, first appearing in Philadelphia in 1759, originally was designed to minimize the loss from death by pooling the risk with others. Accident insurance appeared in the United States in the mid-1800s, and automobile insurance appeared in the late 1800s. Today, the general categories of insurance include life, health, property, liability, suretyship, package, and social.

As the insurance business became more complex, the need for specialized personnel, like claims representatives, developed.

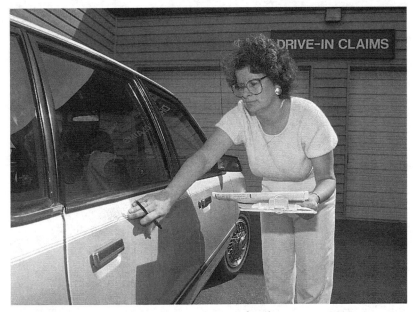

An insurance claims adjuster inspects a car for damage. *(David R. Frazier, The Image Works)*

THE JOB

An insurance company's reputation and success is dependent upon its ability to quickly and effectively investigate claims, negotiate equitable settlements, and authorize prompt payments to policyholders. Insurance employees perform the following duties.

Claims clerks review insurance forms for accuracy and completeness. Frequently, this involves calling or writing the insured party or other people involved to secure missing information. After placing this data in a claim file, the clerk reviews the insurance policy to determine coverage. Routine claims are transmitted for payment; if further investigation is needed, the clerk informs the claims supervisor.

In companies specializing in property and casualty insurance, claims adjusters may perform some or all of the duties of claims clerks. They determine whether the policy covers the loss and amount claimed through a variety of methods. Claims adjusters investigate physical evidence, examine reports and photographs, and secure testimony from relevant parties (via a written statement or recorded audio or video), including the claimant, witnesses, police, and, if necessary, hospital personnel. They occasionally consult with engineers, lawyers, accountants, architects, and construction workers, who can provide expert opinions on the veracity of the claims. If the claim appears justified, the adjuster promptly negotiates a settlement. Adjusters make sure that the settlement reflects the actual claimant losses, while making certain the insurer is protected from invalid claims.

Adjusters may issue payment checks or submit their findings to claims examiners for payment. If litigation is necessary, adjusters recommend this action to legal counsel, and they may attend court hearings.

Most claims adjusters specialize in one type of insurance. They act exclusively in one field, such as fire, marine, automobile, or product liability. A special classification is the *claims agent for petroleum,* who handles activities connected with locating, drilling, and producing oil or gas on private property. In states with "no fault" insurance, adjusters are not concerned with responsibility, but they still must determine the amount of payment. To help settle automobile insurance claims, an *automobile damage appraiser* examines damaged cars and other vehicles, estimates the cost of labor and parts, and determines whether it is more practical to make the repairs on the damaged car or to pay the claimant the precollision market value of the vehicle.

For minor or routine claims, the trend among property and casualty insurers is to employ *telephone* or *inside adjusters.* They use the telephone and written correspondence to gather information, including loss estimates, from the claimant. Drive-in claim centers have developed to provide on-the-spot settlement for minor claims. After determining the loss, the adjuster issues a check immediately.

More complex claims are handled by *outside adjusters.* Outside adjusters spend more time in the field investigating the claim and gathering relevant information.

People who experience a business or residential loss due to vandalism or fire damage may choose to hire a *public adjuster.* These professionals represent the interests of the individuals in negotiations with insurance companies. They investigate the facts of a claim and prepare and present claims to insurance companies with the goal of attaining the highest settlement possible for the individual.

In life and health insurance companies, *claims examiners* perform all the functions of claims adjusters. Examiners in these companies, and in others where adjusters are employed, review settled claims to make sure the settlements and payments adhere to company procedures and policies. They report on any irregularities. In cases involving litigation, they confer with attorneys. Where large claims are involved, a senior examiner frequently handles the case.

If examiners or adjusters believe that fraud has been committed by a claimant, they refer the claim to an *insurance investigator*. Fraud might involve a staged accident, unnecessary medical procedures, arson, or false worker disability claims. The investigator conducts a background check on the claimant to see if he or she has ever been accused or convicted of fraud. Then they interview claimants and witnesses to gather information to verify if the claim is legitimate. The investigator may even conduct surveillance of the individual to determine if his or her actions contradict what was stated in the insurance claim. For example, an individual who claims a back injury caused by workplace activities should not be lifting heavy objects. During surveillance, the investigator may observe the individual helping a friend move, shoveling snow, or working on demanding home remodeling projects. In these instances, the investigator takes video or photographs to document the evidence. He or she then writes a report and passes along the evidence to the insurance company that fraud is occurring. Investigators may testify to their findings in court or during other legal proceedings.

REQUIREMENTS

High School
Recommended high school courses include typing or word processing, computer science, business, and mathematics. Speech and English classes will help you hone your communication skills.

Postsecondary Training
College graduates generally are preferred for insurance claims jobs, but persons with special experience may not need a degree. No specific college major is preferred, but may indicate a possible specialty. For example, an engineering degree would be valuable in industrial claims, and a legal background would be helpful in claims involving workers' compensation and product liability. In most companies, on-the-job training is usually provided. All insurance claims representatives should be comfortable working with computers, so be sure to develop your computer skills in college.

Supplementary professional education is encouraged by insurance companies. A number of options are available.

Certification or Licensing
The Insurance Institute of America offers a series of courses culminating in a comprehensive examination. Passing the exam earns the examinee an associate in claims designation. In addition, life and

health claims examining programs for people interested in working as claims examiners are offered by both LOMA and the International Claim Association; both programs lead to a professional designation.

Most states require claims representatives to be licensed. The requirements for licensing vary and may include age restrictions, state residency, education in such classes as loss adjusting or insurance, character references, and written examinations. Contact your state's department of professional regulation for information on licensing requirements in your state.

Other Requirements

Claims representatives are in a people-oriented profession. They must be able to communicate effectively to gain the respect and confidence of all involved parties. They should be mathematically adept and have a good memory. Knowledge of legal and medical terms and practice, as well as state and federal insurance laws and regulations, is required in this profession. Some companies require applicants to take aptitude tests designed to measure mathematical, analytical, and communication skills.

EXPLORING

There are many ways to explore this field. You might try to get a summer or part-time entry-level job with an insurance company. This would allow you to see what working in the insurance industry is like. You can also ask your parents, teachers, or a school counselor to arrange a tour of an insurance company or at least to set up an information interview with someone who works in the field. Finally, you may consider contacting the various associations that offer educational materials and even sign up for an introductory course to see if this career is for you.

EMPLOYERS

There are approximately 294,600 insurance claims adjusters, examiners, and investigators in the United States. Insurance companies are the principal employers of processing and claims clerks, adjusters, and appraisers. Others are employed by real estate firms and by government agencies.

STARTING OUT

A person interested in this field should contact the personnel departments of insurance companies directly. Positions can also be located in the classified sections of newspapers and on the Internet at industry-related sites.

ADVANCEMENT

Depending upon the individual, advancement prospects are good. As trainees demonstrate competence and advance in course work, they are assigned higher and more difficult claims. Promotions are possible to department supervisor in a field office or a managerial position in the home office. Sometimes claims workers transfer to underwriting and sales departments.

EARNINGS

Salaries for those working in the insurance industry vary according to their position, experience, and education. According to the U.S. Department of Labor (DOL), insurance adjusters, examiners, and investigators averaged $57,130 in 2009. Salaries ranged from less than $34,820 to $85,810 or more. The department also reports that automobile damage appraisers had median annual earnings of $55,390 in 2009. Salaries ranged from less than $37,580 to more than $77,380.

Insurance companies usually offer strong fringe benefits, including liberal vacation policies and employer-financed life and retirement programs. Many companies offer telecommuting options—especially for outside claims adjusters.

WORK ENVIRONMENT

Inside adjusters work in offices, as do clerks and examiners. They work 40 hours a week and occasionally travel. They may work additional hours during peak claim periods or when quarterly or annual reports are due. Outside claims adjusters may travel extensively—sometimes hundreds of miles to different states to handle a claim. An adjuster may also be required to be on call 24 hours a day.

OUTLOOK

Employment in this field will grow about as fast as the average for all careers through 2018, according to the DOL. Most new jobs will be created as a result of increased insurance sales (especially health insurance), resulting in a larger number of insurance claims. Jobs will also come from growth in the population (especially the elderly population, which are making an increasing number of claims), economics, trends in insurance settlement procedures, and opportunities arising from employees who change jobs or retire.

The predominance of the group most in need of protection, individuals between 25 and 54, indicates the need for more claims jobs. Also, as the number of working women rises, so will demand for increased insurance coverage. New and expanding businesses will require insurance for production plants and equipment as well as employees.

Claims representatives who specialize in health insurance, property and casualty insurance (especially in regions of the United States that are prone to natural disasters), complex business insurance (such as marine cargo), workers' compensation, and product and pollution liability insurance, will be in demand. Insurance claims representatives will always be in demand since their work requires significant interpersonal contact and does not lend itself to automation.

FOR MORE INFORMATION

For information on the health insurance industry, contact
America's Health Insurance Plans
601 Pennsylvania Avenue, NW, South Building, Suite 500
Washington, DC 20004-2601
Tel: 202-778-3200
E-mail: ahip@ahip.org
http://www.aahp.org

For information on scholarships and women in the insurance industry, contact
Association of Professional Insurance Women
c/o The Beaumont Group, Inc.
990 Cedar Bridge Avenue, Suite B& PMB 210
Brick, NJ 08723-4157
Tel: 973-941-6024
http://www.apiw.org

For general information about the insurance industry, contact
Insurance Information Institute
110 William Street
New York, NY 10038-3901
Tel: 212-346-5500
http://www.iii.org

For information on the associate in claims designation and other educational programs, contact
Insurance Institute of America/American Institute for CPCU
720 Providence Road, Suite 100
Malvern, PA 19355-3433
Tel: 800-644-2101
E-mail: customerservice@TheInstitutes.org
http://www.aicpcu.org

For information on INVEST, a school-to-work insurance program, and scholarships, contact
Insurance Vocational Education Student Training (InVEST)
127 South Peyton Street
Alexandria, VA 22314-2879
Tel: 800-221-7917
E-mail: info@investprogram.org
http://www.iiaba.net/eprise/main/Invest/Index.html

For information on professional designations, contact
International Claim Association
1155 15th Street, NW, Suite 500
Washington, DC 20005-2725
Tel: 202-452-0143
http://www.claim.org

For information on professional education, contact
LOMA
2300 Windy Ridge Parkway, Suite 600
Atlanta, GA 30339-8443
Tel: 800-275-5662
E-mail: askloma@loma.org
http://www.loma.org

Information on public insurance adjusting can be obtained by contacting the following association:
National Association of Public Insurance Adjusters
21165 Whitfield Place, #105
Potomac Falls, VA 20165-7276
Tel: 703-433-9217
E-mail: info@napia.com
http://www.napia.com

For information on certification and educational programs in Canada, contact

Insurance Institute of Canada
18 King Street East, 16th Floor
Toronto, ON M5C 1C4 Canada
Tel: 416-362-8586
E-mail: iiomail@insuranceinstitute.ca
http://www.insuranceinstitute.ca

Insurance Policy Processing Workers

OVERVIEW

Insurance policy processing workers perform a variety of clerical and administrative tasks that ensure that insurance applications and claims are handled in an efficient and timely manner. They review new applications, make adjustments to existing policies, work on policies that are to be reinstated, check the accuracy of company records, verify client information, and compile information used in claim settlements. Insurance policy processing personnel also handle business correspondence relating to any of the above duties. They use computers, word processors, calculators, and other office equipment in the course of their work. There are approximately 253,800 insurance policy processing workers employed in the United States.

HISTORY

Organized insurance was first developed in the shipping industry during the late 1600s as a means of sharing the risks of commercial voyages. Underwriters received a fee for the portion of the financial responsibility they covered. As the need for further protection developed, other types of insurance were created. After the London Fire of 1666, fire insurance became available in England. Life insurance first appeared in the United States in 1759, accident insurance followed in 1863, and automobile insurance was instituted in 1898.

A clerk files paperwork at an insurance office. *(Bob Daemmrich, The Image Works)*

Now, millions of dollars worth of insurance policies are written every day. Skilled claims examiners, medical-voucher clerks, and other insurance workers are needed to process applications and claims accurately and efficiently so clients get the coverage to which they are entitled.

THE JOB

Insurance policy processing workers are involved in all aspects of handling insurance applications and settling claims (or requests from policy owners regarding payment). The individual policies are sold by an *insurance agent* or *broker,* who sends the policies to processing workers and waits to see whether the company accepts the policy under the terms as written. The agent or the customer may contact policy-processing workers many times during the life of a policy for various services. *Claims examiners* review settled insurance claims to verify that payments have been made according to company procedures and are in line with the information provided in the claim form. These professionals may also need to contact policy processing clerks in the course of reviewing settlements. While a policy processing worker may be assigned a variety of tasks, insurance companies increasingly rely on specialists to perform specific functions.

Claims clerks review insurance claim forms for accuracy and completeness. Frequently, this involves calling or writing the insured party or other people involved to secure missing information. After placing this data in a claims file, the clerk reviews the insurance policy to determine the coverage. Routine claims are transmitted for payment; if further investigation is needed, the clerk informs the claims supervisor.

Claims supervisors not only direct the work of claims clerks but are also responsible for informing policy owners and beneficiaries of the procedures for filing claims. They submit claim liability statements for review by the actuarial department and inform department supervisors of the status of claims.

Reviewers check completed insurance applications to ensure that all questions have been answered by the applicants. They contact insurance agents to inform them of any problems with the applications; if they don't find any problems, reviewers suggest that policies be approved and delivered to applicants. Reviewers may collect premiums from new policy owners and provide management with updates on new business.

Policy-change clerks compile information on changes in insurance policies, such as a change in beneficiaries, and determine if the proposed changes conform to company policy and state law. Using rate books and databases and knowledge of specific types of policies, these clerks calculate new premiums and make appropriate adjustments to accounts. Policy-change clerks may help write a new policy with the client's specified changes or prepare a rider to an existing policy.

Cancellation clerks cancel insurance policies as directed by insurance agents. They compute any refund due and mail any appropriate refund and the cancellation notice to the policy owner. Clerks also notify the bookkeeping department of the cancellation and send a notice to the insurance agent.

Revival clerks approve reinstatement of customers' insurance policies if the reason for the lapse in service, such as an overdue premium, is corrected within a specified time limit. They compare answers given by the policy owner on the reinstatement application with those previously approved by the company, and they examine company records to see if there are any circumstances that make reinstatement impossible. Revival clerks calculate the irregular premium and the reinstatement penalty due when the reinstatement is approved, type notices of company action (approval or denial of reinstatement), and send this notification to the policy owner.

Insurance checkers verify the accuracy and completeness of insurance company records by comparing the computations on premiums paid and dividends due on individual forms. They then check that information against similar information on other applications. They also verify personal information on applications, such as the name, age, address, and value of property of the policy owner, and they proofread all material concerning insurance coverage before it is sent to policy owners.

Insurance agents must apply to insurance companies in order to represent the companies and sell their policies. *Agent-contract clerks* evaluate the ability and character of prospective insurance agents and approve or reject their contracts to sell insurance for a company. They review the prospective agent's application for relevant work experience and other qualifications and check the applicant's personal references to see if they meet company standards. Agent-contract clerks correspond with both the prospective agent and company officials to explain their decision to accept or reject individual applications.

Medical-voucher clerks analyze vouchers sent by doctors who have completed medical examinations of insurance applicants and approve payment of these vouchers based on standard rates. These clerks note the doctor's fee on a form and forward the form and the voucher to the insurance company's bookkeeper or other appropriate personnel for further approval and payment.

REQUIREMENTS

High School
A high school diploma is usually sufficient for beginning insurance policy processing workers. To prepare yourself for this job, you should take courses in English, mathematics, and computer science while in high school. In addition, take as many business-related courses as possible, such as typing, word processing, and bookkeeping.

Postsecondary Training
Community colleges and vocational schools often offer business education courses that provide training for insurance policy processing workers. You may want to consider taking these courses to improve your possibilities for advancement to supervisory positions.

Other Requirements
In order to succeed in this field, you should have some aptitude with business machines and software programs, the ability to concentrate for long periods of time on repetitive tasks, and mathematical skills. Legible handwriting is a necessity. Because you will often work with

policy owners and other workers, you must be able to communicate effectively and work well with others. In addition, insurance policy processing workers need to be familiar with state and federal insurance laws and regulations. They should find systematic and orderly work appealing, and they should like to work on detailed tasks.

Other personal qualifications include dependability, trustworthiness, and a neat personal appearance. Insurance policy processing personnel who work for the federal government may need to pass a civil service examination.

EXPLORING

You can get experience in this field by assuming clerical or bookkeeping responsibilities for a school club or other organization. In addition, some school work-study programs may have opportunities with insurance companies for part-time, on-the-job training. You might also get a part-time or summer job with an insurance company.

You can get training in office procedures and the operation of business machinery and computers through evening courses offered by business schools. Another way to gain insight into the responsibilities of insurance policy processing workers is to talk to someone already working in the field.

EMPLOYERS

Approximately 253,800 insurance claims and policy processing clerks are employed in the United States. Insurance companies are the principal employers of insurance policy processing workers. These workers may perform similar duties for real estate firms and government agencies.

STARTING OUT

If you are interested in securing an entry-level position, you should contact insurance agencies directly. Jobs may also be located through help-wanted advertisements or by visiting industry-related Web sites. Some insurance companies may give you an aptitude test to determine your ability to work quickly and accurately. Work assignments may be made on the basis of the results of this test.

ADVANCEMENT

Many inexperienced workers begin as file clerks and advance to positions in policy processing. Insurance policy processing workers usually begin their employment by handling the more routine tasks, such as reviewing insurance applications to ensure that all the questions have been answered. With experience, they may advance to more complicated tasks and assume a greater responsibility for complete assignments. Those who show the desire and ability may be promoted to clerical supervisory positions, with a corresponding increase in pay and work responsibilities. To become a claims adjuster or an underwriter, it is usually necessary to have a college degree or have taken specialized courses in insurance. Many such courses are available from local business or vocational colleges and various industry trade groups.

The high turnover rate among insurance policy processing workers increases opportunities for promotions. The number and kind of opportunities, however, may depend on the place of employment and the ability, training, and experience of the employee.

EARNINGS

Insurance policy processing workers' salaries vary depending on such factors as the worker's experience and the size and location of the employer. Generally, those working for large companies in big cities earned higher salaries. According to the U.S. Department of Labor (DOL), the median yearly income for insurance policy processing clerks was $34,040 in 2009. Salaries ranged from less than $23,880 to $50,660 or more.

As full-time employees of insurance companies, policy processing workers usually receive the standard fringe benefits of vacation and sick pay, health insurance, and retirement plans.

WORK ENVIRONMENT

As is the case with most office workers, insurance policy processing employees work an average of 37–40 hours a week. Although the work environment is usually well ventilated and lighted, the job itself can be fairly routine and repetitive, with most of the work taking place at a desk. Policy processing workers often interact with other insurance professionals and policyholders, and they may work under close supervision.

Because many insurance companies offer 24-hour claims service to their policyholders, some claims clerks may work evenings and weekends. Many insurance workers are employed part time or on a temporary basis.

OUTLOOK

The DOL predicts little or no employment change for insurance processing workers through 2018. Employment opportunities should be best in and around large metropolitan areas, where the majority of large insurance companies are located. There should be an increase in the number of opportunities for temporary or part-time work, especially during busy business periods. Many jobs will result from workers retiring or otherwise leaving the field.

Increased use of data processing machines and other types of automated equipment will increase worker productivity and may result in the need for fewer workers. Those who continue to improve their skills via continuing education classes and postsecondary study will have the best job prospects.

FOR MORE INFORMATION

For general information about the insurance industry, contact
Insurance Information Institute
110 William Street
New York, NY 10038-3901
Tel: 212-346-5500
http://www.iii.org

For information on educational programs, contact
Insurance Institute of America/American Institute for CPCU
720 Providence Road, Suite 100
Malvern, PA 19355-3433
Tel: 800-644-2101
E-mail: customerservice@theinsitutes.org
http://www.aicpcu.org

For information on insurance careers in Canada, contact
Insurance Institute of Canada
18 King Street East, 16th Floor
Toronto, ON M5C 1C4 Canada
Tel: 416-362-8586
E-mail: iiomail@insuranceinstitute.ca
http://www.insuranceinstitute.ca

Insurance Underwriters

QUICK FACTS

School Subjects
Business
Mathematics

Personal Skills
Following instructions
Leadership/management

Work Environment
Primarily indoors
Primarily one location

Minimum Education Level
Bachelor's degree

Salary Range
$35,630 to $57,820 to
$99,420+

Certification or Licensing
Recommended

Outlook
Decline

DOT
169

GOE
13.02.04

NOC
1234

O*NET-SOC
13–2053.00

OVERVIEW

Insurance underwriters review individual applications for insurance coverage to evaluate the degree of risk involved. They decide whether the insurance company should accept an applicant, and, if the applicant is accepted, underwriters determine the premium that the policyholder will be charged. There are approximately 102,900 underwriters employed in the United States.

HISTORY

Lloyd's of London is generally considered to be the first insurance underwriter. Formed in the late 1600s, Lloyd's subscribed marine insurance policies for seagoing vessels. Over the years, the principles of insurance were adopted by various fraternal and trade unions.

In the United States, fire and life insurance companies date from colonial times. Benjamin Franklin helped start the Philadelphia Contributionship for the Insurance of Houses, a fire insurance company, in 1752. The first life insurance company was established in 1759 by the New York and Philadelphia synods of the Presbyterian Church.

Industrial insurance began in the late 19th century, offering life insurance to millions of industrial workers. In 1910, the first workers' compensation policy was issued. Group coverage was introduced in the life insurance field in 1911, and has since been broadened to include disability, hospitalization, and pension benefits. Group hospitalization insurance was pioneered by the Blue Cross organization in 1936. Private insurance companies began to furnish insurance protection in the early 1900s.

Package insurance, such as automobile and homeowners insurance, which includes a variety of types of insurance, developed on a large scale in the 1950s. Health maintenance organizations were first established during the early 1970s in an attempt to stem the rising cost of health care. Judgments in liability lawsuits had drastically increased by 1980, resulting in rapid growth in purchases of liability insurance. Today, insurance packages and managed care companies provide many options and levels of coverage.

THE JOB

People buy insurance policies to protect themselves against financial loss resulting from injuries, illnesses, or lost or damaged property; policyholders transfer this risk of loss from themselves to their insurance companies. As a result, insurance companies assume billions of dollars in risks each year. Underwriters are responsible for evaluating the degree of risk posed by each policy application to determine whether the insurance company should issue a policy.

Underwriters base their decisions on a number of factors, including the applicant's health, occupation, and income. They use sophisticated computer software to review and analyze information in insurance applications, medical reports, reports from loss control specialists, and actuarial studies. If an applicant appears to be at a greater risk level than normal, the underwriter may decide that an extra premium is needed. Underwriters must exercise sound judgment when deciding whether to accept an applicant and in deciding upon the premium; their decisions are crucial to the financial success of the insurance company.

Insurance underwriting is a very competitive business. If the underwriter evaluates risks too conservatively and quotes prices that are too high, the insurance company may lose business to competitors. If the underwriters evaluate risks too liberally and accept applications at inadequate prices, the company will have to pay more claims and will ultimately lose money. It is essential that underwriters evaluate applications very carefully.

Many underwriters specialize in life, health, mortgage, and property and casualty; many further specialize in individual or group policies. *Property or casualty underwriters* may specialize by the type of risk involved, such as fire or automobile. Some underwriters work exclusively with business insurance. These *commercial account underwriters* must often evaluate the firm's entire business operation.

Group contracts are becoming increasingly popular. In a group policy, life or health insurance protection is given to all persons in a certain group at uniform rates. Group contracts may also be given to specified groups as individual policies reflecting individual needs. A labor union, for example, may be given individual casualty policies covering automobiles.

Underwriters must assess the acceptability of risk from a variety of policy applications. They must be able to review and analyze complex technical information.

REQUIREMENTS

High School

Small insurance companies may hire people without a college degree for trainee positions, and high school graduates may be trained for underwriting work after working as underwriting clerks. In general, however, a college education is advantageous, if not required, for employment. In high school you should take mathematics, business, economics, and speech classes to help prepare you for work in this field. Since most underwriting is done using computer software, it is a good idea to gain as much experience using computers as possible.

Postsecondary Training

Most insurance companies prefer to hire college graduates for beginning underwriting jobs. Many different majors are acceptable, but a degree in business administration or finance may be particularly helpful. Accounting classes and business law classes will help to round out your educational background for this field. In addition, keep up your computer skills in college. You will use computers and the Internet throughout your professional career.

Certification or Licensing

Underwriters who become certified, or designated, show commitment to their profession and increase their possibilities for advancement. Several designations are available to underwriters. The American Institute for Chartered Property Casualty Underwriters (AICPCU) offers the associate in commercial underwriting (AU) designation, which was originally developed by the Insurance Institute of America. Requirements for the AU include completion of designated course work (usually lasting two years) and the passage of a comprehensive examination. The institute also offers a more advanced professional certification, the chartered property and casualty underwriter (CPCU) designation. Certification is also offered by the National Association of Health Underwriters.

For life insurance underwriters, The American College offers the chartered life underwriter (CLU) designation. Like the CPCU, the CLU requires completing a comprehensive series of courses and passing examinations. In addition, the college has teamed up with the National Association of Insurance and Financial Advisors to offer the more extensive life underwriter training council fellow (LUTCF) designation. To receive this certification, individuals must meet or exceed qualifications and continuing education requirements determined by the College. The American College also offers the registered health underwriter designation to underwriters involved in the sale and service of health insurance. Candidates must complete three courses, maintain ethical standards, and satisfy experience requirements.

Other Requirements

Underwriting work requires great concentration and mental alertness. Underwriters must be analytical, logical, and detail oriented. They must be able to make difficult decisions based on technical, complicated information. Underwriters must also be able to communicate well both in speech and in writing. Group underwriters often meet with union employees or employer representatives. The ability to communicate well is vital for these underwriters.

Keep in mind that advancement in this career comes through continuing your education. While insurance companies often pay tuition for their employees taking underwriting courses, the underwriters themselves must have the desire to learn continuously.

EXPLORING

There are many different ways to explore the underwriting profession. You may visit insurance companies to talk with underwriters and other insurance employees. Many insurance associations, such as those listed at the end of this article, offer information on the industry and careers at their Web sites. You might also consider applying for a part-time or summer job at an insurance company. Even if you answer phones or help file records for the office, you are still gaining basic business experience.

High school graduates may decide to work at insurance companies before going to college to determine their interest in and aptitude for underwriting work. In addition, many insurance companies are willing to hire and train college students during the summer months.

EMPLOYERS

Most of the approximately 102,900 underwriters in the United States work for property and casualty insurance companies. Insurance agents, brokers, and services and life insurance companies are the next two largest employers of underwriters. Opportunities are often best in large cities such as New York, Chicago, San Francisco, Dallas, Philadelphia, and Hartford. Finally, some underwriters work in independent agencies, banks, mortgage companies, or regional offices.

STARTING OUT

The most effective way to enter the underwriting profession is to seek employment after earning a college degree. Most insurance companies prefer to hire college graduates, and college career services offices often assist students in securing employment.

It is possible to enter this field without a college degree. Underwriting clerks who show exceptional promise may be trained for underwriter positions. In addition, some insurance companies will hire people without a college degree for trainee jobs.

ADVANCEMENT

Advancement opportunities for underwriters depend on an individual's educational background, on-the-job performance, and leadership abilities. Continuing education is also very important.

Experienced underwriters who have taken continuing education courses may be promoted to chief underwriter or underwriting manager. Underwriting managers may advance to senior management positions.

EARNINGS

According to the U.S. Department of Labor (DOL), underwriters had median earnings of $57,820 in 2009. At the low end of the scale, 10 percent of underwriters earned less than $35,630 per year. The top 10 percent earned $99,420 or more. Experience, certification, and position within the company are all factors influencing salary levels. In addition, most insurance companies provide generous employee benefits, normally including liberal vacation allowances, reimbursement for continuing education, salary incentives, and employer-financed group life and retirement plans.

WORK ENVIRONMENT

Underwriters generally work at a desk in pleasant offices; their jobs entail no unusual physical activity, although at times they may have to work under stressful conditions. The normal workweek is 40 hours; overtime may be required from time to time. Occasionally, underwriters may travel away from home to attend meetings or continuing education classes.

OUTLOOK

The DOL predicts that employment for underwriters will decline slowly through 2018. The increasing use of underwriting software programs and the growing numbers of businesses that self-insure have reduced demand for underwriters. Despite this prediction, employment opportunities will be good because many people are expected to leave the field for other professions or retirement.

There will always be a need for underwriters. New businesses will seek protection for new plants and equipment, insurance for workers' compensation, and product liability. The public's growing security consciousness and the increasing importance of employee benefits will result in continuing opportunities in this field. And, finally, the increasing number of Americans over the age of 65 who utilize long-term health care insurance and pension benefits will create a demand for underwriters. The DOL predicts that "job opportunities should be best for those with experience in related insurance jobs, a background in finance, and strong computer and communication skills."

FOR MORE INFORMATION

For information regarding the LUTCF and CLU designations and distance education programs, contact
The American College
270 South Bryn Mawr Avenue
Bryn Mawr, PA 19010-2105
Tel: 610-526-1000
http://www.theamericancollege.edu

For information regarding the AU and CPCU certifications, contact
American Institute for Chartered Property Casualty
  Underwriters/Insurance Institute of America
720 Providence Road, Suite 100
Malvern, PA 19355-3433

Tel: 800-644-2101
E-mail: cserv@cpcuiia.org
http://www.aicpcu.org

For information on scholarships and women in the insurance industry, contact
Association of Professional Insurance Women
c/o The Beaumont Group, Inc.
990 Cedar Bridge Avenue, Suite B& PMB 210
Brick, NJ 08723-4157
Tel: 973-941-6024
http://www.apiw.org

For general information about the insurance industry, contact
Insurance Information Institute
110 William Street
New York, NY 10038-3901
Tel: 212-346-5500
http://www.iii.org

For information on INVEST, a school-to-work insurance program, and scholarships, contact
Insurance Vocational Education Student Training (InVEST)
127 South Peyton Street
Alexandria, VA 22314-2879
Tel: 800-221-7917
E-mail: info@investprogram.org
http://www.iiaba.net/eprise/main/Invest/Index.html

For general information about health underwriting, contact
National Association of Health Underwriters
2000 North 14th Street, Suite 450
Arlington, VA 22201-2573
Tel: 703-276-0220
E-mail: info@nahu.org
http://www.nahu.org

For information on life underwriting, contact
National Association of Insurance and Financial Advisors
2901 Telestar Court
Falls Church, VA 22042-1205
Tel: 877-866-2432
http://www.naifa.org

This organization is associated with The American College and has information on industry news and events.

Society of Financial Service Professionals
19 Campus Boulevard, Suite 100
Newtown Square, PA 19073-3239
Tel: 610-526-2500
http://www.financialpro.org

Life Insurance Agents and Brokers

QUICK FACTS

School Subjects
Business
Mathematics

Personal Skills
Communication/ideas
Leadership/management

Work Environment
Primarily indoors
One location with some
travel

Minimum Education Level
Some postsecondary training

Salary Range
$25,800 to $45,500 to
$114,910+

Certification or Licensing
Voluntary (certification)
Required by all states
(licensing)

Outlook
About as fast as the average

DOT
250

GOE
10.02.02

NOC
6231

O*NET-SOC
41–3021.00

OVERVIEW

Life insurance agents and brokers sell policies that provide life insurance, retirement income, and various other types of insurance to new clients or to established policyholders. Some agents are referred to as *life underwriters*, since they may be required to estimate insurance risks on some policies. Approximately 434,800 insurance agents and brokers work in the United States.

HISTORY

The first life insurance company in the United States was founded in Philadelphia in 1759 and was known as "A Corporation for the Relief of Poor and Distressed Presbyterian Ministers and of Poor and Distressed Widows and Children of Presbyterian Ministers." The company did business into the 1990s (under the shortened name of Presbyterian Ministers Fund), until it was acquired by Provident Life Insurance Company. In the middle of the 19th century, companies similar to today's life insurance firms began to develop. Two types of organizations grew: mutual companies, which are owned by the policyholders, and stock companies, which are owned by stockholders. The emergence of the profession of full-time insurance agent, who is paid a commission on the basis of what is sold, contributed greatly to the growth of life insurance.

THE JOB

Life insurance agents act as field sales representatives for the companies to which they are under contract. They may be under direct contract or work through a general agent who holds a contract. Insurance brokers represent the insurance buyer and do not sell for a particular company but place insurance policies for their clients with the company that offers the best rate and coverage. In addition, some brokers obtain several types of insurance (automobile, household, medical, and so on) to provide a more complete service package for their clients.

The agent's work may be divided into five functions: identifying and soliciting prospects, explaining services, developing insurance plans, closing the transaction, and following up.

The life insurance agent must use personal initiative to identify and solicit sales prospects. Few agents can survive in the life insurance field by relying solely on contacts made through regular business and social channels. They must make active client solicitation a part of their regular job. One company, for example, asks that each agent make between 20 and 30 personal contacts with prospective customers each week, through which eight to 12 interviews may

An insurance agent (right) reviews an insurance policy with a client. *(David Young-Wolff, Photo Edit)*

Top 10 U.S. Life/Health Insurance Groups and Companies (by revenue, 2009)

1. MetLife
2. New York Life Insurance
3. Prudential Financial
4. TIAA-CREF
5. Massachusetts Mutual Life Insurance
6. Northwestern Mutual
7. AFLAC
8. Unum Group
9. Guardian Life Insurance Company of America
10. Lincoln National

Source: Insurance Information Institute

be obtained, resulting in from zero to three sales. As in many sales occupations, many days or weeks may pass without any sales, and then several sales in a row may suddenly develop.

Some agents obtain leads for sales prospects by following newspaper reports to learn of newcomers to the community, births, graduations, and business promotions. Other agents specialize in occupational groups, selling to physicians, farmers, or small businesses. Many agents use general telephone or mail solicitations to help identify prospects. The emergence of the Internet has changed the insurance business. Today, customers are able to conduct research about life insurance policies and obtain quotes on the Internet. Then they contact agents or the insurance company directly to obtain more information and/or purchase a policy. Regardless of the method they use to reach potential clients, all agents hope that satisfied customers will suggest future sales to their friends and neighbors.

Successful contact with prospective clients may be a difficult process. Many potential customers already may have been solicited by a number of life insurance agents or may not be interested in buying life insurance at a particular time. Agents are often hard-pressed to obtain their initial goal—a personal interview to sit down and talk about insurance with the potential customer.

Once they have lined up a sales interview, agents usually travel to the customer's home or place of business. During this meeting, agents explain their services. Like any other successful sales pitch, this explanation must be adapted to the needs of the client. A new father, for example, may wish to ensure his child's college education, while an older person may be most interested in provisions dealing with retirement income. With experience, agents learn how best to answer questions or objections raised by potential customers. The agents must be able to describe the coverage offered by their company in clear, nontechnical language.

With the approval of the prospective client, the agent develops an insurance plan. In some cases, this will involve only a single standard life insurance policy. In other instances, the agent will review the client's complete financial status and develop a comprehensive plan for death benefits, payment of the balance due on a home mortgage if the insured dies, creation of a fund for college education for children, and retirement income. Such plans usually take into account several factors: the customer's personal savings and investments, mortgage and other obligations, Social Security benefits, and existing insurance coverage.

To best satisfy the customer's insurance needs, and in keeping with the customer's ability to pay, the agent may present a variety of insurance alternatives. The agent may, for example, recommend term insurance (the cheapest form of insurance since it may only be used as a death benefit) or ordinary life (which may be maintained by premium payments throughout the insured's life but may be converted to aid in retirement living). In some cases, the agent may suggest a limited payment plan, such as 20-payment life, which allows the insured to pay the policy off completely in a given number of annual premiums. Agents can develop comprehensive life insurance plans to protect a business enterprise (such as protection from the loss resulting from the death of a key partner), employee group insurance plans, or the creation and distribution of wealth through estates. The agent's skill and the variety of plans offered by the company are combined to develop the best possible insurance proposal for customers.

Closing the transaction is probably the most difficult part of the insurance process. At this point, the customer must decide whether to purchase the recommended insurance plan, ask for a modified version, or conclude that additional insurance is not needed or affordable.

After a customer decides to purchase a policy, the agent must arrange for him or her to take a physical examination; insurance company policies require that standard rates apply only to those people in good health. The agent also must obtain a completed insurance application and the first premium payment and send them with other supporting documents to the company for its approval and formal issuance of the policy.

The final phase of the insurance process is follow-up. The agent checks back frequently with policyholders both to provide service and to watch for opportunities for additional sales.

Successful life insurance agents and brokers work hard at their jobs. Because arranging a meeting often means fitting into the client's personal schedule, many of the hours worked by insurance agents are in the evenings or on weekends. In addition to the time spent with customers, agents must spend time in their homes or offices preparing insurance programs for customer approval, developing new sources of business, and writing reports for the company.

REQUIREMENTS

High School

Formal requirements for the life insurance field are few. Because more mature individuals are usually better able to master the complexities of the business and inspire customer confidence, most companies prefer to hire people who are at least 21 years of age. Many starting agents are more than 30 years of age. If this field interests you, there are a number of courses you can take in high school to prepare yourself for college and this type of work. Naturally you should take English classes. These classes will help you improve your research, writing, and possibly speaking skills—all communication skills that you will use in this line of work. Business classes will teach you how to interact professionally with others and deal with customer needs. If your high school offers economics or finance classes, take these as well. Working with insurance means working with money and numbers, and these classes will give you this exposure. You may also benefit from taking sociology and psychology classes, which can give you a greater understanding of people. Finally, take math and computer classes. Undoubtedly you will be using computers in your professional life, so start becoming comfortable with this tool now.

Postsecondary Training

Today most insurance companies and agencies prefer to hire college graduates. Those who have majored in economics or business will likely have an advantage in getting jobs. Classes you can take in college that will help you in this field include math, economics, and accounting. Business law, government, and business administration classes will help you understand the functions of different types of insurance as well as learn how to successfully run a business. Of course, keep up with your computer education. Knowing how to use software, such as spreadsheet software, will be indispensable in your line of work. You may want to attend a college or university that offers specific courses in insurance; there are more than 60 colleges and universities in the United States that offer such classes.

Certification or Licensing

For full professional status, many companies recommend that their agents become chartered life underwriters (CLU) and/or chartered financial consultants (ChFC). To earn these designations, agents must successfully complete at least three years of work in the field and course work offered through The American College (http://www.theamericancollege.edu). This work will demonstrate the agents' ability to apply their knowledge of life insurance fundamentals, economics, business law, taxation, trusts, and finance to common insurance problems. Only a small percentage of life insurance agents are CLUs and/or ChFCs.

Life insurance agents must obtain a license in each state in which they sell insurance. Agents are often sponsored for this license by the company they represent, which usually pays the license fee.

In most states, before a license is issued, the agent must pass a written test on insurance fundamentals and state insurance laws. Companies usually provide training programs to help prepare for these examinations. Often, the new agent may sell on a temporary certificate while preparing for the written examination. Information on state life insurance licensing requirements can be easily obtained from the state commissioner of insurance. Agents who sell securities, such as mutual funds, must obtain a separate securities license.

Other Requirements

Personal characteristics of agents are of great importance. The following traits are most helpful: a genuine liking and appreciation for people; a positive attitude toward others and sympathy for their problems; a personal belief in the value of life insurance coverage; a willingness to spend several years learning the business and becoming established; and persistence, hard work, and patience. Sales workers should also be resourceful and organized to make the most effective use of their time.

Requirements for success in life insurance are elusive, and it is this fact that contributes to the high turnover rate in this field. Despite the high rate of failure, life insurance sales offer a rewarding career for those who meet its requirements. It has been said that life insurance offers the easiest way to earn $1,000 to $2,000 a week, but the most difficult way to earn $300 or $400. People with strong qualifications may readily develop a successful insurance career, but poorly qualified people will find it a very difficult field.

EXPLORING

Because of state licensing requirements, it is difficult for young people to obtain actual experience. The most notable exceptions are the student-agency programs developed by several insurance companies to provide college students with practical sales experience and a trial exposure to the field.

To get a general idea of how business transactions take place in the professional world, join or start a business club at your school. You might also be able to get a part-time or summer job as a clerical worker in an insurance agency. This work will provide background information on the requirements for the field and an understanding of its problems and prospects for the future. Formal college or evening school courses in insurance will also provide a clearer picture of this profession's techniques and opportunities.

EMPLOYERS

Life insurance agents and brokers can be found throughout the country, but most work in or near large cities. The majority work out of local offices or in independent agencies or brokerages; others are employed at insurance company headquarters. There are approximately 434,800 insurance agents and brokers working in the United States. Approximately 22 percent of insurance sales agents are self-employed.

STARTING OUT

Aspiring agents may apply directly to personnel directors of insurance companies or managers of branches or agencies. In most cases, the new agent will be affiliated with a local sales office almost immediately. To increase the agency's potential sales volume, the typical insurance office manager is prepared to hire all candidates who can be readily recruited and properly trained. Prospective life insurance agents should discuss their career interests with representatives of several companies to select the employer that offers them the best opportunities to fulfill their goals.

Prospective agents should carefully evaluate potential employers to select an organization that offers sound training, personal supervision, resources to assist sales, adequate financial compensation, and a recognizable name that will be well received by customers. Students graduating from college should be able to arrange campus interviews with recruiters from several insurance companies. People with work experience in other fields usually find life insurance managers eager to discuss sales opportunities.

In addition to discussing personal interests and requirements for success in the field, company representatives usually give prospective agents aptitude tests, which are developed either by their company or by LIMRA International (formerly the Life Insurance Marketing and Research Association).

Formal job training usually involves three phases. In precontract orientation, candidates are provided with a clearer picture of the field through classroom work, training manuals, or other materials. On-the-job training is designed to present insurance fundamentals, techniques of developing sales prospects, principles of selling, and the importance of a work schedule. Finally, intermediate instruction usually provides company training of an advanced nature.

More than 150,000 agents have taken continuing educational courses prepared by The American College. After completing a certain number of courses, an agent may apply for the professional educational designation of life underwriter training council fellow.

ADVANCEMENT

Continuing education has become essential for life insurance agents. Several professional organizations offer courses and tests for agents to obtain additional professional certification. Although voluntary, many professional insurance organizations require agents to commit to continuing education on a regular basis. Membership in professional organizations and the accompanying certification is important in establishing client trust. Many states also require continuing education to maintain licensing.

Unlike some occupations, many of the ablest people in the life insurance field are not interested in advancing into management. There can be many reasons for this. In some cases, a successful sales agent may be able to earn more than the president of the company. Experienced agents often would rather increase their volume of business and quality of service rather than their responsibility for the work of others. Others develop by specializing in various phases of insurance.

Still, many successful agents aspire to positions in sales management. At first, they may begin by helping train newcomers to the field. Later, they may become assistant managers of their office. Top agents are often asked by their companies (or even by rival insurance companies) to take over as managers of an existing branch or to develop a new one. In some cases, persons entering management must take a temporary salary cut, particularly at the beginning, and may earn less than successful agents.

There are several types of life insurance sales office arrangements. *Branch office managers* are salaried employees who work for their company in a geographic region. *General agency managers* are given franchises by a company and develop and finance their own sales office. *General agents* are not directly affiliated with their company, but they must operate in a responsible manner to maintain their right to represent the company. *General insurance brokers* are self-employed persons who place insurance coverage for their clients with more than one life insurance company.

The highest management positions in the life insurance field are in company headquarters. Persons with expertise in sales and field management experience may be offered a position with the home office.

EARNINGS

According to the U.S. Department of Labor (DOL), in 2009 the median yearly income of insurance agents and brokers was $45,500. The department also reported that the lowest paid 10 percent of these workers, which typically includes those just beginning in the field, made less than $25,800. The highest paid 10 percent earned $114,910 or more. Many offices also pay bonuses to agents who sell a predetermined amount of coverage. Beginning agents usually receive some form of financial assistance from the company. They may be placed on a moderate salary for a year or two; often the amount of salary declines each month on the assumption that commission income on sales will increase. Eventually, the straight salary is replaced by a drawing account—a fixed dollar amount that is advanced each month against anticipated commissions. This account helps agents balance out high- and low-earning periods.

Agents receive commissions on two bases: a first-year commission for making the sale (usually 55 percent of the total first-year premium) and a series of smaller commissions paid when the insured pays the annual premium (usually 5 percent of the yearly payments for nine years). Most companies will not pay renewal commissions to agents who resign.

WORK ENVIRONMENT

The job of the life insurance agent is marked by extensive contact with others. Most agents actively participate in groups such as churches, synagogues, community groups, and service clubs, through which they can meet prospective clients. Life insurance agents also have to stay in touch with other individuals to keep their prospective sales list growing.

Because they are essentially self-employed, agents must be self-motivated and capable of operating on their own. In return, the life insurance field offers people the chance to go into business for themselves without the need for capital investment, long-term debt, and personal liability.

When asked to comment on what they liked least about the life insurance field, a group of experienced agents listed the amount of detail work required of an agent, the lack of education by the public concerning life insurance, the uncertainty of earnings while becoming established in the field, and the amount of night and weekend work. The last point is particularly important. Some agents work four nights a week and both days of the weekend when starting out. After becoming established, this may be reduced to three or two evenings and only one weekend day. Agents are often torn between the desire to spend more time with their families and the reality that curtailing evening and weekend work may hurt their income. Most agents work a 40-hour week, although those beginning in the field and those with thriving businesses may work longer, some up to 60 hours.

OUTLOOK

The DOL predicts that employment for insurance agents and brokers will grow about as fast as the average for all careers through 2018. The percentage of citizens older than 65 is growing at a much faster rate than that of the general population. Agents will be needed to meet the special needs of this group, converting some insurance policies from a death benefit to retirement income. Also, the 25-to-54 age group is growing. This is the age group that has the greatest need for insurance, and agents will be needed to provide them with services. In addition, more women in the workplace will increase insurance sales. Finally, employment opportunities for life insurance agents will be aided by the general increase in the nation's population, the heavy turnover among new agents, and the openings created by agents retiring or leaving the field. Opportunities will be strongest for agents who speak a foreign language, for those who use the Internet to market their services, and for those who pursue continuing and advanced education.

A number of factors may limit job growth in this field. For example, some life insurance business has been taken over by multiline insurance agents who handle every type of insurance, thus reducing the need for those specializing in selling life insurance. Department stores and other businesses outside the traditional insurance industry have begun to offer insurance. Also, customer service representatives are increasingly assuming some sales functions, such as expanding accounts and occasionally generating new accounts. Many companies are diversifying their marketing efforts to include some direct mail and telephone sales. Increased use of computers will lessen the workload of agents by creating a database for tailor-made policies. Rising productivity among existing agents also will hold down new job openings. In addition, the life insurance industry has come under increasing competition from financial institutions that offer retirement investment plans such as mutual funds.

FOR MORE INFORMATION

The American College is the nation's oldest distance learning institution for financial service education. For information regarding the CLU and ChFC designations, contact
The American College
270 South Bryn Mawr Avenue
Bryn Mawr, PA 19010-2105
Tel: 610-526-1000
http://www.theamericancollege.edu

For information on scholarships and women in the insurance industry, contact
Association of Professional Insurance Women
c/o The Beaumont Group, Inc.
990 Cedar Bridge Avenue, Suite B& PMB 210
Brick, NJ 08723-4157
Tel: 973-941-6024
http://www.apiw.org

The IIABA is the nation's oldest and largest independent agent and broker association and offers job and consumer information.
Independent Insurance Agents & Brokers of America Inc. (IIABA)
127 South Peyton Street
Alexandria, VA 22314-2879

Tel: 800-221-7917
E-mail: info@iiaba.org
http://www.iiaba.net

For general information about the insurance industry, contact
Insurance Information Institute
110 William Street
New York, NY 10038-3901
Tel: 212-346-5500
http://www.iii.org

For information on INVEST, a school-to-work insurance program, and scholarships, contact
Insurance Vocational Education Student Training (InVEST)
127 South Peyton Street
Alexandria, VA 22314-2879
Tel: 800-221-7917
E-mail: info@investprogram.org
http://www.iiaba.net/eprise/main/Invest/Index.html

For information on insurance aptitude tests, contact
LIMRA International
300 Day Hill Road
Windsor, CT 06095-1783
Tel: 800-235-4672
http://www.limra.com

For information on continuing education, contact
National Association of Insurance and Financial Advisors
2901 Telestar Court
Falls Church, VA 22042-1205
Tel: 877-866-2432
http://www.naifa.org

The following organization represents independent professional insurance agents. Visit its Web site for more information.
National Association of Professional Insurance Agents
400 North Washington Street
Alexandria, VA 22314-2366
Tel: 703-836-9340
E-mail: web@pianet.org
http://www.pianet.org

This society is a professional organization consisting of graduates from The American College and other professionals in the insurance and finance fields.

Society of Financial Service Professionals
19 Campus Boulevard, Suite 100
Newtown Square, PA 19073-3239
Tel: 610-526-2500
http://www.financialpro.org

For information on insurance careers in Canada, contact
Insurance Institute of Canada
18 King Street East, 16th Floor
Toronto, ON M5C 1C4 Canada
Tel: 416-362-8586
E-mail: iiomail@insuranceinstitute.ca
http://www.insuranceinstitute.ca

Loan Officers and Counselors

OVERVIEW

Loan officers help individuals or businesses secure loans from financial institutions. They screen potential clients and assist them in the paperwork needed to apply for a loan. Loan officers gather personal and credit information, and use this information to gauge the chance of loan repayment. They may specialize in commercial, consumer, or mortgage loans. *Loan counselors* provide guidance to those individuals or businesses that have qualification problems. In such cases, they may suggest appropriate loans and explain any special requirements or restrictions. Loan officers and counselors may work for banks, mortgage companies, or credit unions. In some institutions, loan officers and counselors may have interchangeable duties. There are approximately 327,800 loan officers and counselors employed in the United States.

HISTORY

The Continental Congress chartered the first bank of the United States, the Bank of North America, in 1781. It was established to print money, purchase securities (stocks and bonds) in companies, and lend money. It was at this time that the career of financial institution loan officer and counselor originated—although the bank owner or his family probably handled these tasks.

QUICK FACTS

School Subjects
Business
Mathematics

Personal Skills
Communication/ideas
Leadership/management

Work Environment
Primarily indoors
Primarily one location

Minimum Education Level
Bachelor's degree

Salary Range
$31,030 to $54,880 to
  $105,330+ (loan officers)
$26,630 to $37,320 to
  $61,210+ (loan counselors)

Certification or Licensing
Recommended

Outlook
About as fast as the average
  (loan officers)
Faster than the average (loan
  counselors)

DOT
186

GOE
13.02.04

NOC
0122

O*NET-SOC
13–2071.00, 13–2072.00

Facts About the Banking Industry, 2008

- Approximately 1.8 million people were employed in the U.S. banking industry. Commercial banks provided 74 percent of positions, with the remainder of workers employed by savings institutions and credit unions.
- Approximately 64.5 percent of workers in the banking industry were employed in office and administrative support jobs; 25.2 percent in management, business, and financial occupations; and 4.1 percent in professional and related occupations.
- Approximately 8 percent of workers in the industry (mostly tellers) worked part time.
- Employment in the banking industry is expected to grow by 8 percent from 2008 to 2018—more slowly than the average for all industries.

Source: U.S. Department of Labor

More than 220 years later, loan officers and counselors continue to play a key role in the banking industry, overseeing trillions of dollars of commercial, consumer, and mortgage loans. Technology has changed the way loan officers and counselors do their jobs. Today, customers can learn about loan options and be pre-approved for loans via the Internet, and loan officers and counselors use computers, databases, e-mail, and other technology to make the loan process easier for consumers. The number of banks and other financial institutions has grown extensively in the past 25 years, and loan officers and counselors will continue to be needed to help run the banking industry.

THE JOB

For most people, financial loans are necessary to make major purchases such as an automobile or house, construction or renovation of an existing home, or to finance a college education. Companies often take out loans to set up a new business, or gain capital to expand an established business. They turn to different financial institutions such as banks, credit unions, or mortgage companies. Loan officers and counselors act as liaisons for the financial institution and the client.

Loan officers may specialize in commercial, consumer, or business loans, or, depending on the size of the lender, handle all types of loans. The loan process usually starts with an initial interview between the loan officer and client. At this time, the type and size of the loan is determined. The loan officer then gathers personal

A loan officer explains loan documents to a couple seeking a home loan. *(Superstock/Photo Library)*

information necessary to complete the application, such as the client's educational background, work history, assets, and credit history. The credit history is important because it often gauges the client's ability to repay the loan. Loan officers can obtain a computerized credit "score" from several reliable sources. If the loan officer is working with a commercial loan, they must also gather the company's financial statements.

Once the information is gathered and verified to be true, then the loan officer meets with loan manager and/or loan underwriter to determine if the loan should be granted or denied. Upon approval, the loan officer notifies the client, and sets up a repayment schedule, or in cases of a mortgage loan, a closing time.

Loan counselors work with clients or businesses that may have problems qualifying for a loan. They find alternate types of loans to best fit the needs of the client, and explain any restrictions or special requirements. They may also help the client set up collateral in order to qualify for the loan. For example, in order to approve a new business loan, the lender may ask the client to offer a home or other asset as collateral in case they fail to repay the loan. Upon default of the loan, the asset may be sold in order to fulfill repayment.

Frequently, loan officers and loan counselors may have many responsibilities that overlap. This is especially true in cases of smaller lending institutions. Loan officers and counselors often act as salespeople. They may make cold calls, or act on sales leads in order to attract new business. Some loan officers, especially those who specialize in consumer loans, may have established relationships with their clients, often working to secure additional loans as the business grows.

Loan officers and counselors have to keep abreast of new developments in the industry. Depending on their training and experience, they may study potential loan markets to develop loan prospects. They also have to learn new computer software used to obtain credit history, be aware of any new tax laws regarding loans, and take sales training or certification classes as required by their place of employment.

REQUIREMENTS

High School

You will need at least a bachelor's degree if you want to work as a loan officer or counselor. While you are in high school, therefore, you should take classes that will give you a solid preparation for college. Such classes include mathematics, such as algebra and geometry, science, history, and a foreign language. Take English courses to improve your researching, writing, and communication skills. Also, take computer classes. Computer technology is an integral part of today's financial world, and you will benefit from being familiar with this tool. Finally, if your high school offers classes in economics, accounting, or finance, be sure to take these courses. The course work will not only give you an opportunity to gain knowledge but will also allow you to see if you enjoy working with numbers and theories.

Postsecondary Training
Possible majors for you in college include accounting, economics, finance, or business administration with an emphasis on accounting or finance. You will need to continue honing your computer skills during this time. Also, you will probably have exposure to business law classes. It is important for you to realize that federal and state laws regarding business and finances change, so you will need to familiarize yourself with current regulations.

Many financial management and banking associations offer continuing education programs in conjunction with colleges or universities. These programs are geared toward advancing and updating your knowledge of subjects such as changing banking regulations, financial analysis, and consumer and mortgage lending.

Certification or Licensing
Certification is one way to show your commitment to the field, improve your skills, and increase your possibilities for advancement. The Mortgage Bankers Association offers the certified mortgage banker (CMB) designation, which has the following areas of expertise: residential or commercial. Those who earn both the residential and commercial designations may apply for the master CMB designation. A fast-track executive CMB designation is available to experienced professionals who can substitute real world experience for aspects of the residential and commercial CMB programs. The association also offers the following specialist designations: commercial mortgage servicing, residential mortgage servicing, residential loan officer, and residential underwriting. There are also three achievement certificates available: mortgage compliance, residential quality assurance, and residential mortgages. The National Association of Credit Management offers business credit professionals a three-part certification program that consists of work experience and examinations. Financial managers pass through the level of credit business associate to credit business fellow to certified credit executive.

Other Requirements

In the banking business, the ability to get along well with others is essential. You should be able to show tact and convey a feeling of understanding and confidence. Honesty is perhaps the most important qualification for this job. Loan officers and counselors have access to confidential financial information about the individuals and business concerns associated with their institutions. Therefore, if you are interested in this career, you must have a high degree of personal integrity.

EXPLORING

Except for high school courses that are business oriented, you will find few opportunities for experience and exploration during high school. Ask your teacher or counselor to arrange a class tour of a financial institution. This will at least give you a taste of how banking services work. You can gain the most valuable experience by finding a part-time or a summer job in a bank or other institution that sometimes hires qualified high school or college students. Finally, to gain some hands-on experience with managing money, consider joining a school or local club in which you could work as the treasurer.

EMPLOYERS

There are approximately 327,800 loan officers and counselors in the United States. They primarily work for commercial banks, savings institutions, credit unions, and mortgage and consumer finance companies.

STARTING OUT

One way to enter banking as a regular employee is through part-time or summer employment. Anyone can apply for a position by writing to a financial institution officer in charge of personnel or by arranging for an interview. Many institutions advertise in the classified section of local newspapers. The larger banks recruit on college campuses. An officer will visit a campus and conduct interviews at that time. Student career services offices can also arrange interviews.

ADVANCEMENT

There is no one method for advancement among loan officers and counselors. Advancement depends on the size of the institution, the services it offers, and the qualifications of the employee. Usually it takes longer to advance when working for smaller employers.

Financial institutions often offer special training programs that take place at night, during the summer, and in some special instances during scheduled working hours. People who take advantage of these opportunities usually find that advancement comes more quickly. The American Banking Institute (part of the American Bankers Association), for example, offers training in every phase of banking through its own facilities or the facilities of the local universities and banking organizations. The length of this training may vary from six months to two years. Years of service and experience are required for a top-level financial institution officer to become acquainted with policy, operations, customers, and the community. Similarly, the National Association of Credit Management offers training and instruction.

EARNINGS

Those who enter banking in the next few years will find their earnings to be dependent on their experience, the size of the institution, and its location. In general, starting salaries in financial institutions are not usually the highest, although among larger financial institutions in big cities, starting salaries often compare favorably with salaries in large corporations.

Loan officers earned median annual salaries of $54,880 in 2009, according to the U.S. Department of Labor (DOL). The lowest paid 10 percent of loan officers made approximately $31,030, while the highest paid 10 percent earned $105,330 or more. Loan counselors earned salaries that ranged from less than $26,630 to $61,210 or more in 2009, with a median salary of $37,320.

Group life insurance, paid vacations, profit-sharing plans, and health care and retirement plans are some of the benefits offered to loan officers and counselors.

WORK ENVIRONMENT

Working conditions in financial institutions are generally pleasant. They are usually clean, well maintained, and often air-conditioned. They are generally located throughout cities for the convenience of both customers and employees. Working hours for financial institution loan officers and counselors may be somewhat irregular, as many organizations have expanded their hours of business.

OUTLOOK

Employment for loan officers is expected to grow about as fast as the average for all occupations through 2018, according to the DOL. Loan counselors should see faster than average growth during this same period. The recent economic crisis has caused a large number of banks to close or be taken over by other banks or the Federal Deposit Insurance Corporation. Additionally, high unemployment rates have made the public wary of taking on unnecessary financial obligations such as car or home loans. This has resulted in fewer employment opportunities for loan officers and counselors. Since most loan officers work on commission, the decline in the real estate market has reduced earnings in the field.

In the future, advances in the way people apply for loans could also spell employment woes. While computerized credit scoring, online mortgage shopping, and online loan applications may increase the efficiency of a loan officer, unfortunately they may also cut the number of professionals needed to get the job done.

College graduates, or those with work experience in lending, banking, or sales, will have the best employment opportunities.

FOR MORE INFORMATION

This organization has information about the banking industry and continuing education available through the American Institute of Banking. It also has information on the Stonier National Graduate School of Banking.

American Bankers Association
1120 Connecticut Avenue, NW
Washington, DC 20036-3902
Tel: 800-226-5377
http://www.aba.com

For certification, industry news, and career information, contact
Association for Financial Professionals
4520 East West Highway, Suite 750
Bethesda, MD 20814-3574
Tel: 301-907-2862
http://www.afponline.org

For information on education, certification, and employment opportunities, contact

Mortgage Bankers Association
1717 Rhode Island Avenue, NW, Suite 400
Washington, DC 20036-3023
Tel: 202-557-2700
http://www.mbaa.org

For information on certification, continuing education, and general information on the banking and credit industry, contact
National Association of Credit Management
8840 Columbia 100 Parkway
Columbia, MD 21045-2158
Tel: 410-740-5560
http://www.nacm.org

Property and Casualty Insurance Agents and Brokers

QUICK FACTS

School Subjects
Business
Mathematics
Speech

Personal Skills
Communication/ideas
Leadership/management

Work Environment
Primarily indoors
Primarily one location

Minimum Education Level
Some postsecondary training

Salary Range
$25,800 to $45,500 to
$114,910+

Certification or Licensing
Recommended (certification)
Required by all states
(licensing)

Outlook
About as fast as the average

DOT
250

GOE
10.02.02

NOC
6231

O*NET-SOC
41–3021.00

OVERVIEW

Property and casualty insurance agents and brokers sell policies that help individuals and companies cover expenses and losses from such disasters as fires, burglaries, traffic accidents, and other emergencies. These salespeople also may be known as *fire, casualty,* and *marine insurance agents or brokers.* There are approximately 434,800 insurance agents and brokers employed in the United States.

HISTORY

The development of the property and casualty insurance industry parallels the history of human economic development. This type of insurance was first established in the maritime field. A single shipwreck could put a ship owner out of business, so it became essential for trade financiers to share this risk. Organized maritime insurance began in the late 17th century at Lloyd's coffeehouse in London, where descriptions of individual ships, their cargoes, and their destinations were posted. Persons willing to share the possible loss, in return for a fee, signed their names below these descriptions indicating what percentage of the financial responsibility they were willing to assume. Those who signed were known as "underwriters," a term still used in the insurance business.

As people became more experienced in this procedure, predictions of loss became more accurate and rates were standardized. To provide protection for larger risks, individuals organized companies. The first marine insurance company in the United States—the Insurance Company of North America—was founded in Philadelphia in 1792 and still does business today (as CIGNA).

Other types of insurance developed in response to people's need for protection. Insurance against loss by fire became available after the disastrous lesson of the London Fire of 1666. The first accident insurance policy in the United States was sold in 1863. Burglary insurance—protection against property taken by forced entry—was offered soon thereafter. Theft insurance, which covers any form of stealing, was first written in 1899.

Around the turn of the century, the development of the "horseless carriage" led to the automobile insurance industry. The first automobile policy was sold in 1898. This area of the insurance field grew rapidly.

Growth of business and industrial organizations required companies to offer protection for employees injured on the job. The first workers' compensation insurance was sold in 1910.

Insurance companies have always been alert to new marketing possibilities. In the past few decades, increasing emphasis has been placed upon "package" policies offering comprehensive coverage. A typical package policy is the homeowner's policy, which, in addition to fire protection for the insured's home and property, also covers losses for liability, medical payments, and additional living expenses. In the mid-1950s, a group of private firms provided the first insurance on the multimillion-dollar reactors used in atomic energy plants.

Over the course of the past decade, costs associated with the property and casualty insurance industry (including underwriting losses) have outstripped the annual rate of inflation. This has generally led to an increase in the premium rates charged to customers. The overall trend reflects some basic changes in American society, including a substantial rise in crime and litigation and the development of expensive new medical technologies. The main challenge of the property and casualty insurance industry in the coming years is to stabilize premium rates to remain competitive with alternative forms of risk financing.

THE JOB

Property and casualty insurance salespeople work as either agents or brokers. An agent serves as an authorized representative of an

Facts About the Insurance Industry, 2008

- Approximately 2.3 million people were employed in the U.S. insurance industry. Insurance carriers provided 61 percent of jobs, with insurance agencies, brokerages, and providers of other insurance-related services employing most of the remaining workers.

- Forty-two percent of workers in the insurance industry were employed in office and administrative support jobs; 20 percent in management or business and financial operations occupations; 17 percent in sales and related careers; and 11 percent in professional and related occupations.

- Employment in the insurance industry overall is expected to grow by 3 percent from 2008 to 2018—more slowly than the average for all industries.

Source: U.S. Department of Labor

insurance company. A broker, on the other hand, serves as the representative for the client and has no contracts with insurance companies.

Agents can be *independent agents, exclusive agents,* or *direct writers.* Independent agents may represent one or more insurance companies, are paid by commission, are responsible for their own expenses, and own the rights to the policies they sell. Exclusive agents represent only one insurance company, are generally paid by commission, are generally responsible for all of their own expenses, and usually own the rights to the policies that they sell. Direct writers represent only one insurance company, are employees of that company (and therefore are often paid a salary and are not responsible for their own expenses), and do not own the rights to the policies that are owned by the company.

Regardless of the system that is used, salespeople operate in a similar fashion. Each one orders or issues policies, collects premiums, renews and changes existing coverage, and assists clients with reports of losses and claims settlement. Backed by the resources of the companies that they represent, individual agents may issue policies insuring against loss or damage for everything from furs and automobiles to ocean liners and factories.

Agents are authorized to issue a "binder" to provide temporary protection for customers between the time the policy application is signed and the policy is issued by the insurance company. Naturally, the agent must be selective in the risks accepted under a binder. Sometimes a risk will be refused by a company, which might cause the agent to lose goodwill with the customer. Because brokers do not directly represent or have contracts with insurance companies, they cannot issue binders.

Some agents or brokers specialize in one type of insurance such as automobile insurance. All agents or brokers, however, must be aware of the kind of protection required by their clients and the exact coverage offered by each company that they represent.

One of the most significant aspects of the property and casualty agent's work is the variety encountered on the job. An agent's day may begin with an important conference with a group of executives seeking protection for a new industrial plant and its related business activities. Following this meeting, the agent may proceed to the office and spend several hours studying the needs of the customer and drafting an insurance plan. This proposal must be thorough and competitively priced because several other local agents will likely be competing for the account. While working at the office, the agent usually receives several calls and visits from prospective or current clients asking questions about protection, policy conditions, changes, or new developments.

At noon, the agent may attend a meeting of a service club or have lunch with a policyholder. After lunch, the agent may visit a garage with a customer to discuss the car repairs needed as the result of the client's automobile accident. Back at the office, the agent may talk on the telephone with an adjuster from the insurance company involved.

In the late afternoon, the agent may call on the superintendent of schools to discuss insurance protection for participants and spectators at athletic events and other public meetings. If the school has no protection, the agent may evaluate its insurance needs and draft a proposed policy.

Upon returning to the office, the agent may telephone several customers, respond to the day's mail, and handle other matters that have developed during the day. In the evening, the agent may call on a family to discuss insurance protection for a new home.

REQUIREMENTS

High School

Insurance companies typically insist that their agents have at least a high school diploma, and most strongly prefer their agents have a college education. There are a number of classes you can take in high school to prepare yourself both for college and for working in the insurance industry. If your high school offers business, economics, or finance classes, be sure to take advantage of these courses. Mathematics classes will also give you the opportunity to develop your skills working with numbers, which is an important aspect of insurance work. Computer science courses will allow you to become familiar with software, hardware, databases, and the Internet. In order to develop your communication skills—essential for any salesperson—take English and speech classes. Finally, consider taking classes that will give you insight into people's actions, which is another important skill for a salesperson. Psychology and sociology classes are courses that may offer this opportunity.

Postsecondary Training
Although college training is not a prerequisite for insurance work, those who have a college degree in economics or business will probably have an advantage starting out in this field. Many colleges and universities offer courses in insurance, and a number of schools offer a bachelor's degree in insurance. Classes you are likely to take in college include finance, accounting, and economics. Business law and business administration classes will give you an understanding of legal issues and insurance needs. Also, psychology courses may help you to increase your understanding of people. Finally, continue to become familiar with computers and the Internet. Courses that teach you to use software, such as spreadsheet programs, will keep your skills up-to-date and make you more marketable. For some specialized areas of property insurance, such as fire protection for commercial establishments, an engineering background may prove helpful.

Certification or Licensing
Those agents who wish to seek the highest professional status may pursue the designation of chartered property casualty underwriter (CPCU). To earn the designation, agents must complete at least three years in the field successfully, demonstrate high ethical practices in all work, and pass a series of examinations offered by the American Institute for Chartered Property and Casualty Underwriters (AICPCU). Agents and brokers may prepare for these examinations by taking courses offered by colleges, insurance associations, or individual companies online or at on-site locations. In 2003, AICPCU introduced a new eight-exam CPCU program that allows agents to specialize in either personal or commercial insurance.

The National Alliance for Insurance Education and Research (http://www.scic.com) also offers the certified insurance counselor and certified insurance service representative designations to agents and brokers who complete short seminars about issues in the field. Contact the alliance for more information.

All agents and brokers must obtain licenses from the states in which they sell insurance. Most states require that the agent pass a written examination dealing with state insurance laws and the fundamentals of property and casualty insurance. Often, candidates for licenses must show evidence of some formal study in the field of insurance.

Other Requirements

An agent or broker must thoroughly understand insurance fundamentals and recognize the differences between the many options provided by various policies. This knowledge is essential to gain the respect and confidence of clients. To provide greater service to customers and increase sales volume, beginning agents must study many areas of insurance protection. This requires an analytical mind and the capacity for hard work.

Successful agents and brokers are able to interact with strangers easily and talk readily with a wide range of people. For example, an agent or broker may need to talk with teenagers about their first cars, with business executives faced with heavy responsibilities, or with widows confronted for the first time with financial management of a home. Agents and brokers must be resourceful, self-confident, conscientious, and cheerful. As in other types of sales occupations, a strong belief in the service being sold helps agents to be more successful in their presentations.

Because they spend so much of their time with others, agents and brokers must have a genuine liking for people. Equally important is the desire to serve others by providing financial security. To be successful, they must be able to present insurance information in a clear, nontechnical fashion. They must be able to develop a logical sales sequence and presentation style that is comfortable for prospects and clients.

Successful agents and brokers may participate in community and service activities to stay visible within their communities and to maintain or increase their volume of business. Agents and brokers often have an unusual facility for recalling people's names and past conversations they've had with them.

EXPLORING

Because of state licensing requirements, it is difficult for young people to obtain part-time experience in this field. Summer employment of any sort in an insurance office may give you helpful insights into the field. Because many offices are small and must have someone on premises during business hours, you may find summer positions with individual agencies or brokerage firms. Colleges with work-study programs may offer opportunities for practical experience in an insurance agency. Finally, ask a school counselor to arrange an information interview with an insurance agent.

EMPLOYERS

Approximately 434,800 insurance agents and brokers are employed in the United States. Insurance companies are the principal employers; however, some agents and brokers (approximately 22 percent of all insurance salespeople) are self-employed.

STARTING OUT

College graduates are frequently hired through campus interviews for salaried sales positions with major companies. Other graduates secure positions directly with local agencies or brokerages through placement services, employment offices, or classified advertisements in newspapers. Many high school and college graduates apply directly to insurance companies. Sometimes individuals employed in other fields take evening or distance education courses in insurance to prepare for employment in this field.

Once hired, the new agent or broker uses training materials prepared by the company or by industry trade groups. In smaller agencies, newcomers may be expected to assume most of the responsibility for their own training by using the agency's written resources and working directly with experienced agents. In larger organizations, initial training may include formal classroom instruction and enrollment in education programs such as those offered by the American Institute for Chartered Property and Casualty Underwriters. Sometimes insurance societies sponsor courses designed to help the beginning agent. Almost all agents receive directed, on-the-job sales supervision.

ADVANCEMENT

Sales agents may advance in one of several ways. They may decide to establish their own agency or brokerage firm, join or buy out an established agency, or advance into branch or home office management with an insurance company.

Self-employed agents or brokers often remain with the organization that they have developed for the length of their careers. They may grow professionally by expanding the scope of their insurance activities. Many agents expand their responsibilities and their office's sales volume by hiring additional salespeople. Occasionally an established agent may enter related areas of activity. Many property insurance agents, for example, branch out into real estate sales. Many agents and brokers devote an increasing amount of their time to worthwhile community projects, which helps to build goodwill and probable future clients.

EARNINGS

Recently hired sales agents are usually paid a moderate salary while learning the business. After becoming established, however, most agents are paid on the basis of a commission on sales. Agents who work directly for an insurance company often receive a base salary in addition to some commission on sales production. Unlike life insurance agents, who receive a high first-year commission, the property and casualty agent usually receives the same percentage each time the premium is paid.

In 2009, all insurance sales agents (including property and casualty) earned a median salary of $45,500 a year, according to the U.S. Department of Labor (DOL). The lowest paid 10 percent earned $25,800 or less, and the highest paid 10 percent earned $114,910 or more.

Salespeople employed by companies often receive fringe benefits (such as retirement income, sick leave, and paid vacations), whereas self-employed agents or brokers receive no such benefits.

WORK ENVIRONMENT

Property and casualty insurance agents must be in constant contact with people—clients, prospective clients, and the workers in the home office of the insurance companies. This can be very time-consuming, and occasionally frustrating, but it is an essential element of the work.

Two of the biggest drawbacks to this type of work are the long hours and the irregular schedule. Agents often are required to work their schedules around their clients' availability. Especially in their first years in the business, agents may find that they have to work three or four nights a week and one or two days on the weekend. Most agents work 40 hours a week, but some agents, particularly those just beginning in the field and those with a large clientele, may work 60 hours a week or more.

OUTLOOK

Employment for insurance agents and brokers is expected to grow about as fast as the average for all occupations through 2018, according to the DOL. Individuals with determination, a college degree, and the right skills (strong sales ability, excellent interpersonal skills, and fluency in a foreign language, especially Spanish) should have numerous job opportunities for several reasons. Demand for insurance should be steady as the general population grows and the amount of personal and corporate possessions increases. Most homeowners and business executives budget insurance as a necessary expense. In addition, laws that require businesses to provide workers' compensation insurance and car owners to obtain automobile liability protection help to maintain an insurance market.

A number of factors, however, are responsible for restraining job growth of insurance agents and brokers. Computers enable agents to perform routine clerical tasks more efficiently, and more policies are being sold by mail and phone. Also, as insurance becomes more and more crucial to their financial health, many large businesses are hiring their own risk managers, who analyze their insurance needs and select the policies that are best for them.

There is a high turnover in this field. Many beginning agents and brokers find it hard to establish a large, profitable client base, and they eventually move on to other areas in the insurance industry. Many openings will occur as a result of this turnover and as workers retire or leave their positions for other reasons.

FOR MORE INFORMATION

For information regarding the CPCU designation, continuing education courses, and industry news, contact
American Institute for Chartered Property and Casualty
    Underwriters/Insurance Institute of America
720 Providence Road, Suite 100
Malvern, PA 19355-3433
Tel: 800-644-2101
E-mail: cserv@cpcuiia.org
http://www.aicpcu.org

For information on scholarships and women in the insurance industry, contact
Association of Professional Insurance Women
c/o The Beaumont Group, Inc.
990 Cedar Bridge Avenue, Suite B& PMB 210
Brick, NJ 08723-4157
Tel: 973-941-6024
http://www.apiw.org

For information on the industry and education programs, contact
Independent Insurance Agents and Brokers of America Inc.
127 South Peyton Street
Alexandria, VA 22314-2879
Tel: 800-221-7917
E-mail: info@iiaba.org
http://www.iiaba.net

For general information about the insurance industry, contact
Insurance Information Institute
110 William Street
New York, NY 10038-3901
Tel: 212-346-5500
http://www.iii.org

For information on INVEST, a school-to-work insurance program, and scholarships, contact
Insurance Vocational Education Student Training (InVEST)
127 South Peyton Street
Alexandria, VA 22314-2879
Tel: 800-221-7917
E-mail: info@investprogram.org
http://www.iiaba.net/eprise/main/Invest/Index.html

Risk Managers

OVERVIEW

Risk managers help businesses control risks and losses while maintaining the highest production levels possible. They work in industrial, service, nonprofit, and public sector organizations. By protecting a company against loss, the risk manager helps it to improve operating efficiency and meet strategic goals.

HISTORY

Entrepreneurs have always taken steps to prevent losses or damage to their businesses. During the Industrial Revolution, business owners recognized that as production levels increased, risks increased at the same rate. The risks were often managed at the expense of worker health and safety.

Only since the mid-1950s, however, has risk management developed into a specialized field. With the rapid growth of technology came greater and more varied risks. Risk management changed from simply buying insurance against risks to planning a wide variety of programs to prevent, minimize, and finance losses.

THE JOB

Risk management protects people, property, and inventory. For example, factories that use hazardous chemicals require employees to wear protective clothing; department stores use closed-circuit surveillance to minimize shoplifting and vandalism; and manufacturers have a plan of action to follow should their products injure consumers. The five general categories of risks are damage to property, loss of income from property damage, injury to others, fraud or criminal acts, and death or injury of employees.

Risk managers first identify and analyze potential losses. They examine the various risk management techniques and select the best ones, including how to pay for losses that may occur. After the chosen techniques are implemented, they closely monitor the results.

Risk management has two basic elements: risk control and risk finance. Risk control involves loss prevention techniques to reduce the frequency and lower the severity of losses. Risk managers make sure operations are safe. They see that employees are properly trained and that workers have and use safety equipment. This often involves conducting safety and loss prevention programs for employees. They make recommendations on the safe design of the workplace and make plans in case of machinery breakdowns. They examine company contracts with suppliers to ensure a steady supply of raw materials.

Risk finance programs set aside funds to pay for losses not anticipated by risk control. Some losses can be covered by the company itself; others are covered by outside sources, such as insurance firms. Risk finance programs try to reduce costs of damage or loss, and include insurance programs to pay for losses.

Large organizations often have a risk management department with several employees who each specialize in one area, such as employee-related injuries, losses to plant property, automobile losses, and insurance coverage. Small organizations have risk managers who may serve as safety and training officers in addition to handling workers' compensation and employee benefits.

REQUIREMENTS
High School
If you are interested in becoming a risk manager, you should plan on getting a bachelor's degree and may at some point consider getting an advanced degree, such as master's of business administration (MBA) or a master's in risk management degree. In high school, therefore, you should take classes that will prepare you for college as well as help you explore this type of work. Take plenty of mathematics classes. Also, take accounting, business, and economics if your school offers these classes. To round out your education, take a variety of science, history, government, and computer classes. And of course, take English classes, which will help you hone your research and writing skills and make you ready for college-level work.

Postsecondary Training

Risk managers generally need a college degree with a broad business background. Depending on the college or university you attend, you may be able to major in risk management or insurance. Approximately 100 schools offer courses or degrees in insurance and risk management. If your school does not offer these degrees, consider a major in other management or finance areas, such as accounting, economics, engineering, finance, law, management, or political science. No matter what your particular major, your class schedule will most likely include economics, accounting, and mathematics, such as calculus. It is also important to take computer classes that teach you how to use software programs. Insurance and even banking classes will give you an understanding of these industries and the financial tools they use.

Certification or Licensing

Many organizations require their risk managers to earn the designation associate in risk management (ARM) or certified risk manager. The ARM program is run jointly by the American Institute for Chartered Property Casualty Underwriters and the Insurance Institute of America. You must take courses and pass exams in the following areas: risk assessment, risk control, and risk financing. The institute also offers the associate in risk management for public entities certification for risk managers who are interested in working in the public sector and the associate in risk management-enterprise-wide risk management. The National Alliance for Insurance Education and Research offers the certified risk managers international designation. To earn this designation, you must pass exams in five courses covering all major areas of risk management.

The Risk and Insurance Management Society (RIMS) offers an advanced designation in risk management, the RIMS Fellow. Applicants must satisfy educational and experience requirements.

Other Requirements

Communications skills are important for risk managers. They must regularly interact with other departments, such as accounting, engineering, finance, human resources, environmental, legal, research and development, safety, and security. They must also be able to communicate with outside sources, such as attorneys, brokers, union officials, consultants, and insurance agents.

Risk managers must have analytical and problem-solving skills in order to foresee potential problem situations and recommend appropriate solutions. They must be able to examine and prepare reports on risk costs, loss statistics, cost-versus-benefit data, insurance costs, and depreciation of assets.

Knowledge of insurance fundamentals and risk financing is necessary. Risk managers must know loss-control issues such as employee health, worker and product safety, property safeguards, fire prevention, and environmental protection.

Management skills help risk managers set goals, plan strategies, delegate tasks, and measure and forecast results. Computer skills and familiarity with business law are also very helpful.

EXPLORING

You may wish to ask your family's insurance agent to help you contact a colleague who has commercial accounts and might introduce you to a risk manager for one of their larger clients.

The Risk and Insurance Management Society (RIMS) offers books, monographs, *Public Risk* magazine, education programs, and an annual conference. The Spencer Educational Foundation, affiliated with RIMS, provides annual scholarships to academically outstanding full-time students of risk management and insurance. (See the end of this article for contact information.)

EMPLOYERS

Airlines, banks, insurance companies, manufacturers, government agencies, municipalities, hospitals, retailers, school districts, nonprofit organizations, colleges and universities, and other organizations employ risk managers.

STARTING OUT

College career services offices can put students in touch with recruiters from industries that employ risk managers. Recent graduates can also send their resumes to employers of risk managers, such as corporations, service providers, government agencies, and other public and private organizations. Some risk managers join insurance companies, insurance brokerage firms, or consulting firms that provide risk management services to clients.

Some individuals gain experience and education while working in accounting or personnel departments and later move into risk management positions.

ADVANCEMENT

There is good potential for advancement in the risk management field. Many risk managers work in a related field, such as in a human resources department handling employee benefits.

Risk managers may eventually head a personnel or finance department, become a human resources director, or join the insurance industry. Some become independent consultants. Membership in professional associations that offer networking opportunities can lead to better positions in the field.

Risk managers usually hold mid-level management positions and often report to a financial officer. Some, however, become vice presidents or presidents of their organizations.

EARNINGS

Risk managers' salaries vary depending on level of responsibility and authority, type of industry, organization size, and geographic region. The U.S. Department of Labor (DOL), which classifies risk managers with financial managers, reported a median yearly income for financial managers of $101,190 in 2009. The lowest paid 10 percent had earnings of less than $54,760, while the highest paid 10 percent earned more than $166,400.

Risk managers usually receive benefits, bonuses, paid vacation, health and life insurance, pensions, and stock options.

WORK ENVIRONMENT

Risk managers work in a variety of settings from schools, stores, and government agencies to manufacturers and airlines. Most work in offices, not on the production line, but they may be required to spend some time in production departments. They may have to travel to study risks in other companies or to attend seminars.

Risk managers usually work a 40-hour week, Monday through Friday. They may have to spend much of their time at a computer, analyzing statistics and preparing reports.

OUTLOOK

Since advanced technology continues to increase productivity as well as the potential for disaster, the need for risk management will continue to grow. Organizations now recognize risk management as an integral and effective tool for cost-containment. The profession will continue to gain recognition in the next decade, so salaries and career opportunities are expected to continue to escalate. The DOL predicts that employment for financial managers (including risk managers) will grow about as fast as the average through 2018.

FOR MORE INFORMATION

For information about the associate in risk management designation, contact

American Institute for Chartered Property Casualty Underwriters/Insurance Institute of America
720 Providence Road, Suite 100
Malvern, PA 19355-3433
Tel: 800-644-2101
E-mail: customerservice@TheInstitutes.org
http://www.aicpcu.org

For information on education, research, and publications, contact
American Risk and Insurance Association
716 Providence Road
Malvern, PA 19355-3402
Tel: 610-640-1997
E-mail: aria@TheInstitutes.org
http://www.aria.org

For information about the certified risk manager designation, contact
National Alliance for Insurance Education and Research
PO Box 27027
Austin, TX 78755-2027
Tel: 800-633-2165
E-mail: alliance@scic.com
http://www.scic.com

Visit the association's Web site for a risk management glossary and other resources.
Public Risk Management Association
500 Montgomery Street, Suite 750
Alexandria, VA 22314-1558
Tel: 703-528-7701
E-mail: info@primacentral.org
http://www.primacentral.org

For information on continuing education and the Spencer Educational Foundation, contact
Risk and Insurance Management Society
1065 Avenue of the Americas, 13th Floor
New York, NY 10018-0713
Tel: 212-286-9292
http://www.rims.org

Tax Preparers

OVERVIEW

Tax preparers prepare income tax returns for individuals and small businesses for a fee, for either quarterly or yearly filings. They help to establish and maintain business records to expedite tax preparations and may advise clients on how to save money on their tax payments. There are approximately 95,800 tax preparers employed in the United States.

HISTORY

President Franklin D. Roosevelt once said, "Taxes are the dues that we pay for the privileges of membership in an organized society." Although most people grumble about paying income taxes and filling out tax forms, everyone carries a share of the burden, and it is still possible to keep a sense of humor about income taxes. As Benjamin Franklin succinctly said, "In this world nothing can be said to be certain, except death and taxes."

While the personal income tax may be the most familiar type of taxation, it is actually a relatively recent method of raising revenue. To raise funds for the Napoleonic Wars between 1799 and 1816, Britain became the first nation to collect income taxes, but a permanent income tax was not established there until 1874. In the same manner, the United States first initiated a temporary income tax during the Civil War. It wasn't until 1913, however, with the adoption of the 16th Amendment to the Constitution, that a tax on personal income became the law of the nation. In addition to the federal income tax, many states and cities have adopted income tax laws. Income taxes

QUICK FACTS

School Subjects
Business
Mathematics

Personal Skills
Following instructions
Helping/teaching

Work Environment
Primarily indoors
Primarily one location

Minimum Education Level
Some postsecondary training

Salary Range
$17,680 to $30,060 to
$64,270+

Certification or Licensing
Voluntary (certification)
Required by certain states
(licensing)

Outlook
More slowly than the
average

DOT
219

GOE
13.02.03

NOC
1431

O*NET-SOC
13–2082.00

A tax preparer (left) reviews a client's financial documents. (*Rogelio V. Solis, AP Photo*)

are an example of a "progressive tax," one that charges higher percentages of income as people earn more money.

Technology has now made it possible to file taxes electronically. Electronically filed tax returns are more accurate than paper filed returns because of the extensive checking performed by the electronic filing software. Detecting and correcting errors early also allows the tax return to flow smoothly through the Internal Revenue Service (IRS), speeding up the refund process. In 2010, more than 96 million individual tax returns were e-filed, according to the IRS. Computer software is also available that assists individuals with preparing and filing their own taxes.

THE JOB

Tax preparers help individuals and small businesses keep the proper records to determine their legally required tax and file the proper forms. They must be well acquainted with federal, state, and local tax laws and use their knowledge and skills to help taxpayers take the maximum number of legally allowable deductions.

The first step in preparing tax forms is to collect all the data and documents that are needed to calculate the client's tax liability. The client has to submit documents such as tax returns from previous years, wage and income statements, records of other sources of income, statements of interest and dividends earned, records of expenses, property tax records, and so on. The tax preparer then interviews the client to obtain further information that may have a bearing on the amount of tax owed. If the client is an individual taxpayer, the tax preparer will ask about any important investments, extra expenses that may be deductible, contributions to charity, and insurance payments; events such as marriage, childbirth, and new employment are also important considerations. If the client is a business, the tax preparer may ask about capital gains and losses, taxes already paid, payroll expenses, miscellaneous business expenses, and tax credits.

Once the tax preparer has a complete picture of the client's income and expenses, the proper tax forms and schedules needed to file the tax return can be determined. While some taxpayers have very complex finances that take a long time to document and calculate, others have typical, straightforward returns that take less time. Often the tax preparer can calculate the amount a taxpayer owes, fill out the proper forms, and prepare the complete return in a single interview. When the tax return is more complicated, the tax preparer may have to collect all the data during the interview and perform the calculations later. If a client's taxes are unusual or very complex, the tax preparer may have to consult tax law handbooks and bulletins.

Computers are the main tools used to figure and prepare tax returns. The tax preparer inputs the data onto a spreadsheet, and the computer calculates and prints out the tax form. Computer software can be very versatile and may even print up data summary sheets that can serve as checklists and references for the next tax filing.

Tax preparers often have another tax expert or preparer check their work, especially if they work for a tax service firm. The second tax preparer will check to make sure the allowances and deductions taken were proper and that no others were overlooked. They also make certain that the tax laws are interpreted properly and that calculations are correct. It is very important that a tax preparer's work is accurate and error-free, and clients are given a guarantee covering additional taxes or fines if the preparer's work is found to be incorrect. Tax preparers are required by law to sign every return they complete for a client and provide their Social Security number or federal identification number. They must also provide the client with a copy of the tax return and keep a copy in their own files.

REQUIREMENTS

High School

Although there are no specific postsecondary educational requirements for tax preparers, you should certainly get your high school diploma. While you are in high school there are a number of classes you can take that will help prepare you for this type of work. You should take mathematics classes. Accounting, bookkeeping, and business classes will also give you a feel for working with numbers and show you the importance of accurate work. In addition, take computer classes. You will need to be comfortable using computers, since much tax work is done using this tool. Finally, take English classes. English classes will help you work on your research, writing, and speaking skills—important communication skills to have when you work with clients.

Postsecondary Training

Once you have completed high school, you may be able to find a job as a tax preparer at a large tax-preparation firm. These firms, such as H&R Block and Jackson Hewitt Tax Service, typically require their tax preparers to complete a training program in tax preparation. If you would like to pursue a college education, many universities offer individual courses and complete majors in the area of taxation. Another route is to earn a bachelor's degree or master's degree in business administration with a minor or concentration in taxation. A few universities offer master's degrees in taxation.

In addition to formal education, tax preparers must continue their professional education. Both federal and state tax laws are revised every year, and the tax preparer is obligated to understand these new laws thoroughly by January 1 of each year. Major tax reform legislation can increase this amount of study even further. One federal reform tax bill can take up thousands of pages, and this can mean up to 60 hours of extra study in a single month to fully understand all the intricacies and implications of the new laws. To help tax preparers keep up with new developments, the National Association of Tax Professionals offers more than 200 workshops nationwide every year. Tax service firms also offer classes explaining tax preparation to both professionals and individual taxpayers.

Certification or Licensing

Licensing requirements for tax preparers vary by state, and you should be sure to find out what requirements there are in the state where you wish to practice. Since 2002, for example, tax preparers in California have been required to register with the California Tax Education Council, a nonprofit corporation established by the California State Legislature to oversee tax preparation. Tax preparers who apply for registration in that state must be at least 18 years old. In addition, they need to have 60 hours of formal, approved instruction in basic income tax law, theory, and practice, or two years of professional experience in preparing personal income tax returns. They must complete 20 hours of continuing education each year and always maintain a $5,000 tax preparer bond.

The Internal Revenue Service (IRS) offers an examination for tax preparers. Those who complete the test successfully are called *enrolled agents* and are entitled to legally represent any taxpayer in any type of audit before the IRS or state tax boards. (Those with five years' experience working for the IRS as an auditor or in a higher position can become enrolled agents without taking the exam.) There are no education or experience requirements for taking the examination, but the questions are roughly equivalent to those asked in a college course. The IRS does not oversee seasonal tax preparers, but local IRS offices may monitor some commercial tax offices.

The Institute of Tax Consultants offers an annual open book exam to obtain the title of certified tax preparer. Certification also requires 60 hours of continuing education every two years.

The Accreditation Council for Accountancy and Taxation confers the accredited tax preparer and accredited tax adviser designations to professionals who meet work experience and other requirements. Contact the council for more information.

Other Requirements

Tax preparers should have an aptitude for math and an eye for detail. They should have strong organizational skills and the patience to sift through documents and financial statements. The ability to communicate effectively with clients is critical to be able to explain complex tax procedures and to make customers feel confident and comfortable. Tax preparers also need to work well under the stress and pressure of deadlines. They must also be honest, discreet, and trustworthy in dealing with the financial and business affairs of their clients.

EXPLORING

If a career in tax preparation sounds interesting, you should first gain some experience by completing income tax returns for yourself and for your family and friends. These returns should be double-checked by the actual taxpayers who will be liable for any fees and extra taxes if the return is prepared incorrectly. You can also look for internships or part-time jobs in tax service offices and tax preparation firms. Many of these firms operate nationwide, and extra office help might be needed as tax deadlines approach and work becomes hectic. The IRS also trains people to answer tax questions for its 800-number telephone advisory service; they are employed annually during early spring.

Try also to familiarize yourself with the tax preparation software available on the Internet and utilize Web sites to keep abreast of changing laws, regulations, and developments in the industry. The National Association of Tax Professionals offers sample issues of its publications online. (See the end of this article for contact information.)

EMPLOYERS

Approximately 95,800 tax preparers are employed in the United States. Tax preparers may work for tax service firms that conduct most of their business during tax season. Other tax preparers may be self-employed and work full or part time.

STARTING OUT

Because tax work is very seasonal, most tax firms begin hiring tax preparers in December for the upcoming tax season. Some tax service firms will hire tax preparers from among the graduates of their own training courses. Private and state employment agencies may also have information and job listings, as will classified newspaper ads. You should also consult your school guidance office to establish contacts in the field.

There are a large number of Internet sites for this industry, many of which offer job postings. Most large tax preparation firms, such as H&R Block and Jackson Hewitt Tax Service, also have their own Web sites.

ADVANCEMENT

Some tax preparers may wish to continue their academic education and work toward becoming certified public accountants. Others may want to specialize in certain areas of taxation, such as real estate, corporate, or nonprofit work. Tax preparers who specialize in certain fields are able to charge higher fees for their services.

Establishing a private consulting business is also an option. Potential proprietors should consult with other self-employed practitioners to gain advice on how to start a private practice. Several Internet sites also give valuable advice on establishing a tax business.

EARNINGS

The median annual income for tax preparers was approximately $30,060 in 2009, according to the U.S. Department of Labor (DOL). Salaries ranged from less than $17,680 to more than $64,270 annually. Incomes can vary widely from these figures, however, due to a number of factors. One reason is that tax preparers generally charge a fee per tax return, which may range from $30 to $1,500 or more, depending on the complexity of the return and the preparation time required. Therefore, the number of clients a preparer has, as well as the difficulty of the returns, can affect the preparer's income. Another factor affecting income is the amount of education a tax preparer has. Seasonal or part-time employees, typically those with less education, usually earn minimum wage plus commission. Enrolled agents, certified public accountants, and other professional preparers, typically those with college degrees or more, usually charge more. Finally, it is important to realize that fees vary widely in different parts of the country. Tax preparers in large cities and in the western United States generally charge more, as do those who offer year-round financial advice and services.

Benefits for salaried workers include vacation and sick time, health, and sometimes dental, insurance, and pension or 401(k) plans. Self-employed tax preparers must provide their own benefits.

WORK ENVIRONMENT

Tax preparers generally work in office settings that may be located in neighborhood business districts, shopping malls, or other high-traffic areas. Employees of tax service firms may work at storefront desks or in cubicles during the three months preceding the April 15 tax-filing deadline. In addition, many tax preparers work at home to earn extra money while they hold a full-time job.

The hours and schedules that tax preparers work vary greatly, depending on the time of year and the manner in which workers are employed. Because of the changes in tax laws that occur every year, tax preparers often advise their clients throughout the year about possible ways to reduce their tax obligations. The first quarter of the year is the busiest time, and even part-time tax preparers may find themselves working very long hours. Workweeks can range from as little as 12 hours to 40 or 50 or more, as tax preparers work late into the evening and on weekends. Tax service firms are usually open seven days a week and 12 hours a day during the first three months of the year. The work is demanding, requiring heavy concentration and long hours sitting at a desk and working on a computer.

OUTLOOK

The DOL predicts that employment for tax preparers will grow more slowly than the average for all occupations through 2018. Although tax laws are constantly evolving and people look to tax preparers to save them time, money, and frustration, new tax programs and online resources are easing the process of preparing taxes, lessening the need for outside help. Information is available at the touch of a button on tax laws and regulations. Tax tips are readily available, as are online seminars and workshops.

The IRS currently offers taxpayers and businesses the option to "e-file," or electronically file their tax returns on the Internet. While some people may choose to do their own electronic filing, the majority of taxpayers will still rely on tax preparers—licensed by the IRS as electronic return originators—to handle their returns.

FOR MORE INFORMATION

For information on accreditation, contact
Accreditation Council for Accountancy and Taxation
1010 North Fairfax Street
Alexandria, VA 22314-1574
Tel: 888-289-7763
E-mail: info@acatcredentials.org
http://www.acatcredentials.org

For information on the certified tax preparer designation, contact
Institute of Tax Consultants
7500 212th SW, Suite 205
Edmonds, WA 98026-7617
Tel: 425-774-3521
http://taxprofessionals.homestead.com/welcome.html

For information on becoming certified as an enrolled agent, visit
Internal Revenue Service
U.S. Department of the Treasury
http://www.irs.ustreas.gov

For industry information, contact
National Association of Tax Consultants
321 West 13th Avenue
Eugene, OR 97401-3402

Tel: 800-745-6282
http://www.natctax.org

For information on educational programs and publications, contact
National Association of Tax Professionals
PO Box 8002
Appleton, WI 54912-8002
Tel: 800-558-3402
E-mail: natp@natptax.com
http://www.natptax.com

━━━━━ INTERVIEW ━━━━━

Jill Senso is an enrolled agent and the supervisor of the Tax Knowledge Center for the National Association of Tax Professionals (NATP), a nonprofit membership association of more than 19,500 tax professionals who network together for education, services, and support. Jill's main responsibility at NATP is overseeing the continuing education offerings it provides to the tax professional community. Jill was kind enough to discuss her career and the future of the tax industry with the editors of Careers in Focus: Financial Services.

Q. What is an enrolled agent?

A. An enrolled agent (EA) is a person who has earned the privilege of practicing, that is, representing taxpayers, before the Internal Revenue Service (IRS). Unlike other tax preparers, EAs, like attorneys and certified public accountants, are unrestricted as to which taxpayers they can represent, what types of tax matters they can handle, and which IRS offices they can practice before. I became an EA by passing a stringent two-day, four-part test administered by the IRS. Taxpayers are wise to use the services of an EA because of the extensive level of training and the EA's ability to represent the taxpayer in the event of an audit.

Q. How long have you been a tax practitioner?

A. I have been a tax practitioner for 12 years. I majored in accounting at St. Norbert College and received my B.B.A. I started my career at ArthurAndersen in the tax department, where I tried every area of taxation. I eventually specialized in ArthurAndersen's Federal Business Practice division, where I concentrated on corporate and partnership returns. Over time, however, I realized that I wanted to move back to the community where I grew up. ArthurAndersen did not have an office in this location, so I took a position in the tax department of a regional firm in my community. After focusing my tax career on compliance, I thought that finding a position doing tax research would be a great new learning experience. I took a tax research position with the NATP and have been here ever since.

Q. Why did you decide to become a tax practitioner?

A. As previously stated, I majored in accounting during college. Accounting majors typically interview for jobs the fall before graduation (accounting firms do not have time to do massive amounts of interviews during tax season). I had a number of offers from firms and chose ArthurAndersen. At the national firms, you are hired and can then choose if you would like to work in the tax or audit department. I chose tax mainly because I wanted to travel but not all of the time like the audit team members did. Hence, my career in tax began.

Q. What do you like most and least about your job?

A. What I like most about my job is variety. I get to split my time amongst tax research, writing, proofreading, and facilitating online tax courses. My days go by very quickly. Tax law is ever-changing, so I learn new things every day by reading the various rulings and tax court cases that are released on a daily basis. I also love the interaction I have with NATP members and my clients. It's a great feeling to tell someone you found a way for them to save tax dollars on their tax return.

I guess what I like least about my job are the hours during tax season. Between the drastic increase in research questions I receive and my part-time job doing returns, I do not have much time for anything else. I spend my weekends working. However, I live in Wisconsin, so it's not a bad time of the year to be cooped up in an office. Plus, my income increases as a result of my hard work. Since I don't have time to spend it, I have a nice chunk of money saved once tax season is over. And once tax season is over, things slow down, and my hours during the summer are great (as is the weather in Wisconsin).

One thing I think is important to note is that a career in tax is great for a stay-at-home parent who is looking for some supplemental income but would like summers off. You could either do taxes out of your home from February 1 to April 15, or there are many tax preparation businesses looking for seasonal help. You could choose to work full-time during the tax season or just part-time (e.g., two to three days a week). Many people find that this arrangement blossoms into a rewarding career once their children are grown or begin school. On the other side of the spectrum, many retirees choose tax preparation as a second career. They like the extra income and love only having to work three-and-a-half months of the year.

Q. What advice would you give to high school students who are interested in careers in the tax profession?

A. I would advise enrolling in any business courses offered at your high school. Typing is strongly recommended as well (although I would advise this to anyone regardless of profession); it just saves time, and as the old cliché goes, "Time is money." Do not limit yourself to all business courses, however. Take some elective courses such as art, psychology, and foreign languages. It is always good to be well rounded. In the tax profession, you meet so many different people; it is great if you can hold conversations other than those related to tax and finance. Golf lessons wouldn't hurt either. You get invited to many golf outings, and clients love it when you take them out for a round of golf. I can't guarantee it will make you a great golfer, but you will understand the terminology and should be able to get through nine holes without wanting to crawl in one of them. Contrary to the stereotype that has been cast on accountants, we don't just sit at a desk counting beans all day.

Q. What are the best ways to land a job as a tax practitioner and build a successful business?

A. A great start to become a tax practitioner is to become educated on preparing taxes. There are organizations out there (NATP being one of them) that provide basic tax training for those starting a career in tax preparation. Some employers will pay for you to get the training you need so you can prepare taxes for them. An accounting degree helps in obtaining a career in tax preparation, but isn't necessary. However, if you plan to prepare corporate or partnership returns, strong knowledge of accounting and bookkeeping will give you a huge advantage.

Q. What are the most important professional qualities for tax practitioners?

A. The most important quality for a tax professional is to be ethical. It is your obligation to prepare your clients' taxes according to laws set forth in the Internal Revenue Code. As these laws are incredibly complex and not widely understood by the general public, it is the tax professional's responsibility to comply with these laws and not put their clients in jeopardy of violating them. Of course, other details are important as well. A tax professional should be someone who is very detail oriented and whose reading comprehension allows for him or her to fully understand the rules and regulations as they pertain to taxes. I also advise that those looking for a tax professional ask what continuing education their tax preparer goes to in order to stay current with tax law. Also check to see if they are a member of a professional organization, such as the NATP.

Q. What are the benefits of membership in professional associations such as the National Association of Tax Professionals?

A. Belonging to an established and respected professional association such as the NATP is critical in this age when clients are looking for reassurances of ethical practices. Membership with the NATP connects preparers to the services of a large, full-time, highly trained staff—something they don't often have on their own. The NATP supports members in a variety of career-enhancing ways: research services, high-quality education, products, networking opportunities with others in the industry, support, information, and it joins your voice with a collective voice in expressing industry concerns to the government. As a member of an association, preparers do not need to do everything alone. Communications regarding tax law are analyzed, prioritized, and put into understandable terms so individuals do not need to spend hours deciphering complex information themselves. Associations help keep members on track and attuned to important industry occurrences. People do not join associations for the sake of spending money. They join for the sake of belonging to something larger that assists them to efficiently conduct business. The NATP holds its members to a code of ethics and professional standards, which gives greater assurance to clients. The NATP markets to a broad audience and provides marketing tools for its members to use, being far more effective than the reach of a small office. The NATP develops and delivers high-quality classes presented in hands-on, practical methods that are easy to learn from and apply. There is so much more as well, but it essentially comes down to the power of an association being greater than shouting alone in the dark.

Q. What is the future employment outlook for tax professionals?

A. In my opinion, the future outlook in the field of taxation looks great. As I mentioned, tax law is constantly changing. The average taxpayer is not going to keep up on the law; it's easier and wiser to pay someone to do their returns for him or her. It is time-consuming to keep up with law changes; however, it provides tremendous job security for those of us in the field of taxation. There is talk of a simplified tax system, such as a national sales tax instead of income tax. However, in my opinion, it would take a very long time for such a plan to be implemented—the wheels of change on Capitol Hill turn slowly. For more than 10 years now, I have heard talks about flat tax rates and a simplified tax structure, and I do not think we are any closer to it now than we were 10 years ago.

Index

Entries and page numbers in **bold** indicate major treatment of a topic.